THE NAVAL WRECKS OF SCAPA FLOW

PETER L. SMITH

With Foreword by
Commander (retired) Yorck von Reuter

THE
ORKNEY
PRESS

Peter L. Smith has been diving on wrecks for many years, including professional experience. His interest in ships led him first to an apprenticeship at a turbine manufacturers, and then to entry into the Merchant Navy as an engineering officer. He now lives in North Wales, where he is employed in engineering insurance, and makes frequent expeditions to locate new wreck sites in UK coastal waters, as well as returning to the great naval wrecks of Scapa Flow.

Note: The German gun measurements are given in inches throughout. Metric equivalents are given below:

$$12'' = 305\text{mm}$$
$$5.9'' = 150\text{mm}$$
$$3.4'' = 88\text{mm}$$

The Orkney Press Ltd.
12 Craigiefield Park,
St Ola, Kirkwall, Orkney

First published 1989

ISBN 0 907618 20 0

©Text and diagrams Peter L. Smith

Edited by Pam Beasant
Designed by Iain Ashman
Editorial Management Howie Firth

Underwater wreck photographs
©Peter L. Smith

Marine life photographs
©Heriot-Watt University,
    Institute of Offshore Engineering
    Hamish Mair and Robert Forbes

Printed in Orkney by the Kirkwall Press

Cover illustrations show:

Front cover:

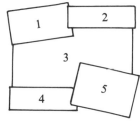

1. 3.4-inch gun, SMS *Köln*
2. HMS *Vanguard* (I.W.M.)
3. Diver in Scapa Flow
4. SMS *Dresden*
   present state
5. Front and port side
   bridge windows and
   signal bridge handrails
   SMS *Brummer*

Back cover:

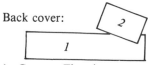

1. German Fleet in
   Scapa Flow, 1918
2. Sea Urchin, Scapa Flow

DEDICATION

In memory of my late father, who stimulated my interest,
to Alan Reece, who sustained it,
and principally, to my wife, Annette, for supporting it.

FOREWORD

by Commander (retired) Yorck von Reuter

(Commander von Reuter is the eldest and only surviving son of Rear-Admiral Ludwig von Reuter who commanded the German High Seas Fleet in internment in Scapa Flow. Commander von Reuter was seven years old when his father returned in January 1920 from captivity in England, following the scuttling of the Fleet. In 1932 he himself entered the Navy, and when war broke out was an officer on a destroyer which took part in the Battle of Narvik in Norway. There he was wounded and captured, and after a period in hospital was a prisoner-of-war in England and then Canada.

After the war, he joined the Navy again in 1956, and during his time in the Fleet Staff was Naval Attache in Turkey. After retirement from the Navy in 1969 he spent thirteen years with the German division of the Shell Oil Company as an adviser for ocean-going tankers. In 1982 he visited Orkney on a cruise ship in the company of retired Admiral Friedrich Ruge, who had been an officer aboard the interned Fleet in Scapa Flow in 1919; their visit included Scapa Flow itself and the Stromness Museum exhibition on the German Fleet.)

> Unser Leben gehet dahin
> wie grosse Schiffe die sinken.
>
> *Our life passes away*
> *like great ships as they sink*

This inscription was found by accident in the vault of Field Marshal Derfflinger (1609-95), in the small village church where he was finally laid to rest. It was found on the 21st June, 1919, the exact day when the battleship SMS *Derfflinger* went to its grave together with the Imperial German Fleet in Scapa Flow.

This year is the 70th anniversary of that happening — a date to be remembered. Newspapers in Germany and the UK have been recording the anniversary, and I am reminded of it by the battle-flag of SMS *Markgraf* which decorates the wall behind my desk.

What led to this unique event in history, when a whole fleet of 74 warships sank themselves within a matter of hours, an action which echoed around the world? On that day, after four years of world war, the peace treaty was to have been agreed upon.

But it turned out to be a day of perplexity rather than joy to both sides. The Armistice had to be prolonged, and it was only on the 28th June, 1919, that the treaty of Versailles was concluded. By this time the German Fleet did not exist any more — it lay on the bottom of Scapa Flow. This fleet had been considered one of the reasons for entering the war, and was to have been divided up amongst the victorious nations.

Grand-Admiral von Tirpitz had built his fleet at the beginning of the 20th century with the idea of 'the unacceptable risk' in mind, that the German Imperial Navy would be so powerful that attack by sea on the German coasts could only be undertaken at considerable risk. This objective was fulfilled, and during that world war those coasts were never threatened; furthermore, any forcing of the straits into the Baltic and thence to Russia was prevented, however much the Allies may have desired it.

After four years of war against the whole world, the strength of the Kaiser's Reich was broken, and along with it the morale of the German Fleet.

My father, Admiral Ludwig von Reuter, as Commander of the interned fleet, took advantage of the fateful occasion to save the Imperial Fleet from the disgrace of surrender. When the Armistice was terminated on 21st June, 1919, he was not informed of the subsequent decision to prolong it, but was convinced that war conditions were reinstated. He then put an end to the fleet in honour by sinking the ships.

Years later, it was found that valuable treasure was covered by the waters of Scapa Flow, and salvage began, which turned out to be a hard job with many problems. Today, several German ships are still on the bottom of Scapa Flow, along with the Royal Naval ships, *Royal Oak* and *Vanguard*. They rest peacefully together on the bottom; the fighting has ended. May this peaceful resting together of the ships of two nations once at war serve as a symbol of lasting concord.

> Was vergangen, kehrt nicht wieder,
> Ging es jedoch leuchtend nieder
> leuchtets lange noch zuruck.

> *What has passed away does not return.*
> *But if it disappeared in glory*
> *its light shines on for long.*

23rd September, 1989.

CONTENTS

ACKNOWLEDGEMENT

My appreciation must be extended to all those divers who
have supported the trips I have organised to Orkney to dive
the majority of the wrecks detailed in this book, and to those
who have put up with me on their own trips. Unfortunately there
are too many to mention individually, but they will know who
they are.

Special thanks are due to John Thornton of Kirkwall,
charter boat operator, and his charming and tolerant wife Linda,
who have afforded me their kind hospitality and invaluable
assistance. Both have become good friends over the years, and
John's knowledge of the German wrecks and of Scapa Flow is
exceptional.

Also to Alan Reece of Bagillt, North Wales, and Peter
Robinson of Rhyl who have read parts of the manuscript and
offered their constructive criticisms; and to Simon Rodger of
Marple, Cheshire for his assistance with obtaining suitable
photographs. All three have been my diving companions on
many occasions and long may it continue.

Peter Rowlands of Ocean Optics, London, has been of great
help in my achieving any underwater photographs. I had not
attempted serious photography in any form, on land or
underwater before the idea for this book evolved in my mind,
and his advice, and loan of a lens for a week on the one
occasion my own had flooded, has allowed me to obtain
reasonably acceptable shots.

My warmest thanks also go to the Institute of Offshore
Engineering of Heriot-Watt University for making available a
selection of the outstanding underwater photographs of marine
life that they have taken in Scapa Flow over the years, as part of

their monitoring of the marine environment of the Flotta oil terminal. As well as the photographers, Hamish Mair and Robert Forbes, warmest thanks go to the Director of the Institute, Prof. Cliff Johnston, and to Ingeborg M. Dickie of the Institute who provided details of the slides and other valued information.

Invaluable assistance with German translations has been given to me by Ilse Antonia Sophia Moody of Mold, North Wales; and when time has been against me typing assistance has been gratefully received from my neighbour Morwenna Griffith and from my brother, Michael who 'lent' me his secretary, Freda McMorine.

I have been extremely privileged to have visited HMS *Royal Oak* and to have attended the Memorial Service and wreath-laying ceremony over the site. This was an honour afforded to me by the Royal Navy and I would thank the Flag Officer, Scotland and Northern Ireland and the Officers of the S. and N.I. Clearance Diving Unit for their permission to join them on these occasions, and to the Clearance Diving Team for their assistance; also the crews of the R.M.A.S. diving support vessels for their hospitality.

The assistance of the Staffs of the Departments of Printed Books and Photographs at the Imperial War Museum, of the Draught Room of the National Maritime Museum and of the Naval Historical Library has been invaluable in my researches.

My thanks and appreciation are due to Mr N. J. M. Campbell and his publishers for their kind permission to use information from Mr Campbell's book *Jutland* published in 1986 by the Conway Maritime Press.

I am also grateful to Dan van der Vat, the author of one of the classic books on the story of the German Fleet, for most kindly making available a copy of one of the original eye-witness accounts of the scuttle.

Finally, I must extend my appreciation to those who have helped in the ultimate creation of this work. To Howie Firth of the Orkney Press for being prepared to 'take the plunge' and publish it; and to Iain Ashman and Pamela Beasant of Stromness for the production in its final form.

The publishers would like to thank Rear Admiral (retired) Dr Werner Schünemann, Rear Admiral (retired) Dieter Hülsemann and Mr Ulrich Maier, for their kind assistance during the final stages of the preparation of this book.

INTRODUCTION

SAILING SOUTH from the old whaling port of Stromness, down the narrow channel of Clestrain Sound between mainland Orkney and the dark heights of the island of Hoy, the gently rolling boat swings her head east round the southern tip of land and into Scapa Flow. The islands part to reveal a calm, blue expanse, fringed in the far distance by the low, grey mounds of Holm, Burray, South Ronaldsay, Flotta and Fara. The names of these humps of islands reveal the origins of modern Orkney. These hospitable waters of Scapa Flow sheltered the fierce Norse warriors, just as in more recent times they became the main anchorage for the mighty leviathans of the British Royal Navy.

These treeless islands and gently lapping shores have borne witness to great historical events; from Norse invasion to the destruction of massive steel warships — creations of later generations of nations still unable to live together in peace. Through wars, piracy and an unshakeable belief in Christianity, the Anglo-Saxon successors to those Norsemen of Great Britain won the greatest Empire ever known. Inevitably, as other nations developed to similar industrial levels, they would rise to challenge Britain's awesome world-wide power, seeking at least a share.

The Federal State of Germany was formed in 1871 under the aristocratic Prussian rule of the Hohenzollerns with Bismarck as the first Chancellor. Each state of the Federation possessed its own army which combined to form the most powerful in the world. It was soon recognised within Germany that the newly-formed nation would also require a navy to support the colonial expansion necessary to the country's development.

Due to inadequate guidance from diplomatic and military

leadership, requirements for the material content of the fleet were in constant debate. The Navy's two components, the Imperial Navy Office and the High Command, could not agree, and the service became something of an embarassment. The Reichstag itself was in permanent turmoil due to its constitutional make-up of social classes, religious, regional, agrarian and industrial factions, not one of which possessed a majority vote.

Through this apparent mayhem rose one Alfred Tirpitz, whose clear vision of Germany's Navy was like a breath of fresh air to Kaiser Wilhelm II, whose ambition it was for Gemany to possess a mighty fleet. Soon after his appointment in March 1897, as State Secretary of the Imperial Navy Office, (and thus the Navy's representative at the Reichstag), Tirpitz wrote a secret memorandum to the Kaiser. He described in detail the future material requirements for a fleet, its function, and how such a fleet could be created. By forcing through as law the types and numbers of ships to be built annually, Tirpitz foresaw that once the building plan was set in motion, the fleet would have to continue to grow to satisfy industrial capacity and public demand.

Tirpitz had risen from the ranks of the Naval Officer corps, and had seen service overseas, witnessing Britain's naval strength and recognising that here was Germany's future enemy. Whilst appreciating that Germany could never build a navy to match Britain's enormous fleet, he was the first strategist to understand that through an arms race, a lever could be applied with which to force another nation in a desired direction. Tirpitz maintained that a powerful German fleet based in the North Sea would deter British attack, and thus Germany's colonial expansion would be uninhibited by fear of reprisals.

After much political intrigue, massive public relations exercises and shrewd use of statistics, Tirpitz succeeded in having his first Navy Law passed through the Reichstag in 1898. Although not fully appreciated then, the ultimate certainty of a war with England was at that time ordained.

History demonstrates that it was the technological advances made during the years to Tirpitz's rise to power, culminating in the ultimate sea weapon of the era — the *Dreadnought*-type battleship — which helped to precipitate the Great War. The first of these, HMS *Dreadnought,* was built by Britain secretly and quickly. She was commissioned in 1905 and immediately rendered obsolete the main fighting units of every maritime power of the world, including her own. Germany was suddenly presented with an opportunity to challenge Britain's command of the seas, and set out to build such ships at a similar pace. The Anglo-German arms race was now in full flight, and the onset of the Great War was only a matter of time.

In the wake of that awful conflict, while the greater part of

Britain's fleet of such ships was dismantled, Germany's finest were scuttled in 1919 and left to rust beneath the waters of Scapa Flow. After their scuttling, they were seen by some purely as a marketable source of scrap metals, a far cry from Tirpitz's dream, and many of them were raised for that purpose after the Great War. At that time, this was all that the ships were worth, as bigger and better vessels were being designed and built. The necessity to do this grew as relations between the Great Powers again deteriorated, and the number of new vessels increased until aircraft and submarine technology rendered the ships vulnerable.

In our present time, however, when none of these mighty ships sail the seas, and none could ever be built again, those that remain on the seabed of Scapa Flow are recognised as more than rusting hulks. They represent not only a milestone in political history, but embody the advances made in engineering and science at the end of the 19th century — particularly in the areas of gunnery science, navigation instruments, power plants and metallurgy.

The scuttling of the German fleet at Scapa Flow was a symptom of the general dissatisfaction felt throughout Germany at the manner of the ending of the Great War. To Britain, however, the German fleet's immolation was the final event of a meticulously planned naval war, where the frustration of distant blockade had been a far more effective weapon than direct confrontation. It had ensured that Britain's deterrent to power-seeking nations, her mighty Royal Navy, had remained intact. Those ships remaining are therefore a monument to a part in Britain's history as important as the Battle of Trafalgar in 1805.

During the Great War, the great natural harbour of Scapa Flow protected the British Grand Fleet from U-boat attack. Strategically, it also afforded the Fleet swift access across the northern sector of the North Sea through which Germany's merchant ships had to pass, and where any foraging German Naval units could be engaged. Britain's distant blockade of the enemy's ports was only possible because of the geographic position of Scapa Flow, which was a principle factor in the defeat of Germany.

Nowhere else in the world can be found any of the first breed of Dreadnought battleship, all either having been broken up for scrap or sunk in water too deep or too inaccessible to dive. Small wonder then, that divers from all quarters of the world descend the still, clear waters of Scapa Flow to marvel at these ships, the ultimate in technological achievement in their time.

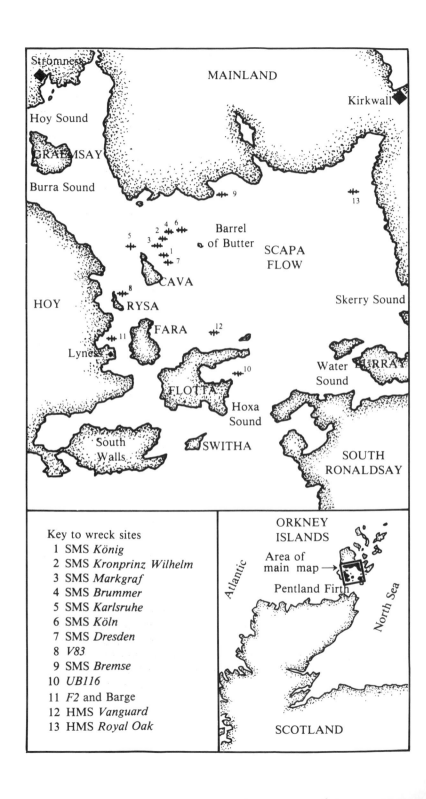

Key to wreck sites
1 SMS *König*
2 SMS *Kronprinz Wilhelm*
3 SMS *Markgraf*
4 SMS *Brummer*
5 SMS *Karlsruhe*
6 SMS *Köln*
7 SMS *Dresden*
8 *V83*
9 SMS *Bremse*
10 *UB116*
11 *F2* and Barge
12 HMS *Vanguard*
13 HMS *Royal Oak*

Chapter 1
AFTERMATH

SEVENTY STEEL WARSHIPS STEAMED in line ahead. There were Dreadought battleships, battlecruisers, cruisers and destroyers with warlike names such as *Hindenburg, Markgraf, Grosser Kurfürst* and *Moltke*. Nineteen miles stretched between the lead ship and the last. Then, out of the early morning mist ahead loomed an even mightier fleet; two parallel rows of over one hundred steel citadels steaming towards the first. Their guns were cleared for action, hulls and upperworks gleaming in pristine splendour. It was a meeting of the two most powerful naval fleets in the world. As they drew abreast, the two lines of the Grand Fleet of the British Royal Navy turned about with impeccable precision, to steam on each side of the Imperial German High Seas Fleet — built solely to challenge the might of Britain's Royal Navy. It was Thursday, 21st November, 1918, two weeks after the end of the First World War. The German Navy, totally defeated and demoralised by blockade, were being brought to internment by their own crews pending the results of the armistice negotiations at Versailles. Disappointed that the German Fleet had not been brought to its knees in battle, Britain hardly recognised that this day was a naval victory as great as Trafalgar.

Germany's naval strategy had been to attempt to entice smaller units of the British Fleet out to battle with larger detachments of their own, to gradually erode the considerable British advantage of numbers. Only then could Germany envisage a successful massed fleet action. Two or three German battlecruisers, for instance, would shell undefended British east coast towns for a short time. (Both Sunderland and Hartlepool suffered civilian casualties during such bombardments). Then,

▲
German
ships
at the
meeting
of the
Fleets
21/11/1918
(Imperial
War
Museum)

5

small detachments of the British battlecruisers based at Rosyth would be dispatched to give chase to the Germans, who, theoretically, would lure the British into the massed German Fleet lying in wait further out in the North Sea. A detachment of British battleships and battlecruisers were almost caught by this ruse early in the war. The German commander, however, mistakenly taking them for the entire Grand Fleet, fled for home.

Whilst en-route to another such action, the Germans did actually run into the whole Grand Fleet. (The British had learned from the earlier engagement not to risk sending out small detachments, and had since backed up their battlecruiser force with battleship squadrons during such sorties). The Commander-in-Chief of the British Fleet, Admiral Jellicoe, had received warning of the impending German action from British intelligence, and had sailed with the whole Grand Fleet to attempt to intercept the enemy. Because bad weather had prevented Zeppelin reconnaissance ahead of their Fleet, the German sortie had been changed to a show of force off the coast of Norway, (who was friendly to Britain), in an attempt to entice the fast British battlecruisers across the North Sea. There they would be met by the supporting German battleships, but at a distance from which these powerful ships would remain unseen from the Norwegian shores.

Thus, on 31st May, 1916, the Fleets met for duel in the furious but indecisive Battle of Jutland. Both Jellicoe, and the German Commander, Admiral Scheer, handled their respective Fleets with great skill, but they had come together late in the afternoon and darkness fell before either side could claim victory. The Germans had sunk three British battlecruisers for the loss of only one of their own, but after the battleships of the Grand Fleet had arrived on the scene, only the stoutness of the German ships prevented heavy losses from the guns of the British Dreadnoughts. Thankful for the smoke and mist created by the boiler fires and cordite explosions, Admiral Scheer made use of the reduced visibility to make for home under the cover of night. The mighty British Grand Fleet — 'Guardian of the British Empire' as described by King George V — had its nose bloodied, but the overall effect was to intimidate the German High Seas Fleet to the extent that, en masse, their ships did not do battle again during the course of the war.

The subsequent blockade of Germany's ports by the Royal Navy had considerable effect upon the war in Europe. As the German Fleet lay idle at its bases in Kiel and Wilhelmshaven, the crews became demoralised. The quality of the provisions deteriorated as few imports could reach Germany, and many men volunteered for U-boat duties to see some action. Those who remained on the big ships grew more restless, and following a number of isolated demonstrations, their anger finally erupted in all-out mutiny during October, 1918. Their action determined the end of the war. The German armies were suffering defeats at the hands of the Allies, and morale throughout the German nation was shattered. The mutineers controlled the naval bases at Kiel and Wilhelmshaven and revolution spread across Germany, forcing the abdication of the Kaiser and the formation of new government.

Against this background, on the afternoon of November 21st, 1918, the crews of the German High Seas Fleet anchored their ships in the Firth of Forth, where they were boarded for inspection by the Royal Navy. On the orders of the British Commander-in-Chief, Admiral Sir David Beatty, (who had succeeded Jellicoe), their ammunition had been landed ashore before sailing, and the breech blocks had been removed from the guns, rendering them useless. The ships were subsequently moved from the Forth to Scapa Flow, there to remain until the politicians had decided their future.

Confined to their ships in the windswept and desolate Scapa Flow, the German crews — bored, cold and miserable — were undisciplined and unkempt. Little maintenance was carried out to their ships; paint peeled off and rust streaks stood out against the once immaculate pale grey hulls. During the next few months, the crews were steadily reduced. Some of the more mutinous were shipped home to ease the task of maintaining order. Others became ill due to the poor quality of food which had to be sent from Germany, and they were sent home too. The British refused any assistance other than the threat of force to subdue the crews, but did give medical attention to those who became seriously ill. Inevitably, a certain amount of fraternisation developed between Orcadian fishermen and some of the Germans. Strictly against orders, schnapps and brandy were exchanged for food and clothes. Men roller-skated on the decks of the big ships, and crews of the smaller ships played tag, scampering around the decks and hiding in gun barbettes and ship's boats. Some fished, and the crew of one torpedo boat caught a seal and shot gulls with a home-made crossbow to supplement their meagre diet.

As the winter of 1918-1919 progressed, conditions on board grew steadily worse. Rats multiplied, and cockroaches became so numerous that they were collected and raced for amusement. Keeping warm became a major problem. The central heating on many ships broke down and due to lack of spares remained redundant. The coal-fired stoves on the cruisers and torpedo boats became dilapidated and inefficient. With the coming of spring, 1919, there was no news of their fate, but the warmer weather and longer daylight made conditions more tolerable as the politicians argued at Versailles.

7

It had been Britain's policy to operate a naval fleet large enough to counter the combined fleets of the two most powerful nations who might have formed an alliance against her. She thus had no desire for the German ships to be handed over to any of her former allies and upset this balance. Both France and Italy would have been delighted to have added the ships to their own fleets, and Germany was ever-hopeful of keeping her navy intact.

The allies finally concluded their armistice terms and handed an ultimatum to Germany to accept by June 21st, 1919, or hostilities would recommence on that day. The terms reduced the German Fleet to a fraction of its former strength. Only six battleships of not more than 10,000 tons were allowed, six cruisers of less than 6,000 tons and twelve torpedo boats — an ineffectual force in world terms. None of the interned ships at Scapa Flow — the most modern units of the German fleet — were to be retained by Germany. The officer commanding the interned fleet, Admiral von Reuter, read this news on June 20th, in a copy of *The Times,* dated June 17th, supplied to him by the British. He was not informed that the deadline for acceptance was later extended until June 23rd. Believing that the peace terms could not be acceptable to Germany, von Reuter assumed that hostilities would recommence on June 21st. Being defenceless, he took the only course open to him, ordering his subordinate officers to scuttle their ships, sinking them at their anchorages.

On the morning of June 21st, the main part of the British Fleet left Scapa Flow for gunnery exercises in the North Sea, they planning secretly to return on June 23rd and seize the German ships.) At 11.00 hours, on a pre-arranged coded signal from their Admiral's Flagship, (the light cruiser *Emden),* his crews set about their tasks. They opened sea cocks, smashed sea water cooling pipes and removed steam condenser covers. Seawater poured in, and as the ships began to sink, the crews took to their boats. Panic spread amongst the small Royal Navy guard force watching over the interned fleet. Attempts were made to force the Germans to return to their ships to stop them from sinking. Rifles and pistols were fired, at first overhead but to no effect, and finally some German officers and men were killed and wounded. A futile event which ought not to have happened. (Placed in identical circumstances, however, any British officer would have acted as von Reuter did, and his crews would have inevitably suffered similar treatment from their guards.) Those who died lie at rest at the Naval Cemetery at Lyness on Hoy, once the British Fleet base. Their graves are to this day as immaculately maintained as those of the many British sailors interred there.

At the time of the scuttling, a party of school-children from the town of Stromness were being conducted on a sight-seeing cruise round the German Fleet, on board a British Fleet tender the *Flying Kestrel*. Their impressions of the huge ships sinking can be well imagined. Hideous screams and roars erupted from the ships as air was forced out of compartments far below the surface, and steam pipes burst on contact with the icy water surging into the hulls. Explosions were heard from deep inside the ships as bulkheads collapsed. As the ships, slowly at first, capsized as stability was lost, heavy machinery was torn by its own weight from its mountings and careered across decks, smashing through partitions and destroying all in its path.

The first ship to slip below the surface at 12.16, was the mighty battleship *Friedrich der Grosse,* Flagship of the Fleet at Jutland. The last to submerge, at 17.00, was the proud battlecruiser, *Hindenburg,* her masts and funnels remaining above the surface as her keel rested on the seabed below. A number of the ships were saved by the British. A battleship *Baden,* some cruisers, *Frankfurt, Emden* and *Nürnberg,* together with eleven torpedo boats were towed close to shore where they settled in shallow water to be ultimately refloated. (These ships were either broken up for scrap or ignominiously used as targets for the warships of the Allied Navies).

Extract from an article by James Taylor — a pupil at Stromness School who witnessed the scuttling.
'On Saturday, June 21st, 1919, I rose very early, as it would never do to be late for a school treat which was to take the form of a cruise on the *Flying Kestrel* to visit the surrendered Geman Fleet . . . the thought of sailing up close to them made us boys almost sick with excitement!

At long last we came face to face with the Fleet . . . Their decks were lined with German sailors who . . . did not seem too pleased to see us.

Suddenly, without any warning and almost simultaneously these huge vessels began to list over to port or starboard; some heeled over and plunged headlong, their sterns lifted high out of the water . . . Out of the vents rushed steam and oil and air with a dreadful roaring hiss.

And as we watched, awestruck and silent, the sea became littered for miles round with boats and hammocks, lifebelts and chests . . . And among it all hundreds of men struggling for their lives.

As we drew away from this nightmare scene we watched the last great battleship slide down with keel upturned, like some monstrous whale.'

After the scuttling, the surface of Scapa Flow was covered with oil and debris from the sunken ships, and it was some years before the Orkney fauna recovered.

The crews of the German ships were rounded up from the islands of Cava and Rysa where many of them had landed, and finally assembled on board HMS *Revenge,* HMS *Royal Oak* and HMS *Resolution.* The German officers were greatly impressed by the immaculate condition of these ships, and by the high standard of discipline on board, having become accustomed to unkempt ships and rebellious crews. The battleships HMS *Revenge* and HMS *Royal Oak,* commissioned only weeks before the Battle of Jutland, were detailed to transport the German crews, now designated prisoners of war, to Invergordon on the Cromarty Firth. During this voyage, many men had personal belongings stolen and were harshly treated by the British crews, who still considered the Germans as enemies. The British authorities were faced with the problem of having to house nearly two thousand men, (although 2,700 had been sent back home only three days before the scuttling). After languishing at Invergordon for a few days, they were transported by rail to Park Hall Prisoner of War camp at Oswestry, Shropshire, suffering abuse on the way from the British public. At Park Hall, the men were allowed to take walks outside the camp and organised football matches. Their physical condition soon improved, and after some months they were moved to Donington Hall near Nottingham, where the accommodation was of a better standard.

The men were finally repatriated to Germany on January 20th, 1920, being held for that time while retribution was demanded from Germany for the loss of the ships. Attempts were made by Britain to prove that von Reuter had destroyed the Fleet on orders from his senior officers in Germany, but without success. Had this been proved, it would have strengthened the Allies' bargaining powers at Versailles, but he was ultimately allowed to return home with his men, where they received a hero's welcome for saving the honour of the German Navy by not allowing the ships to fall into the hands of the enemy.

Apart from those vessels beached and subsequently salvaged, the sunken ships at Scapa Flow were declared a total loss by the British Admiralty, who were no doubt delighted as the ships could no longer be a threat to Britain's naval supremacy. France, however, accused Britain of complicity in the matter. America was unconcerned, fully aware of the financial cost to Britain of the war, and of her own future as the world's leading military power.

Thus the extinguished German Fleet lay unmolested on the bottom of Scapa Flow until 1923, when the Scapa Flow Salvage and Shipbreaking Company was formed to raise some of the torpedo boats. Before they had lifted any, however, one Ernest Cox bought from the Admiralty two of the capital ships, the battlecruisers *Seydlitz,* (lead ship in the shelling of Sunderland

and Hartlepool early in 1916, and the survivor of incredible damage at Jutland), and *Hindenburg,* which must have appeared an attractive purchase as much of her remained above the surface.

In addition, in the name of his company, Cox and Danks Ltd., he bought more than twenty of the torpedo boats lying between Lyness and the island of Cava. Cox was a human dynamo, and his efforts over the next eight years were to become one of the greatest feats of marine salvage ever accomplished.

Using a modified floating dry dock, (ironically handed over by Germany as part of the war reparations), Cox's company lifted twenty-six torpedo boats and broke them up for scrap between August 1924 and April 1926. This in itself was unique in the annals of marine salvage, but was nothing compared to his forthcoming achievements. He had by this time purchased more of the capital ships together with some of the cruisers lying in Scapa Flow.

All of the battleships and battlecruisers (with the exception of *Hindenburg)* had been deliberately capsized as they sank, to prevent any attempts at salvage. It proved, however, to be of considerable help. Cox's divers were sent down first to *Moltke,* a battlecruiser of 22,600 tons and veteran of Jutland. All the holes in her upturned hull were sealed from the inside by men working in compartments made dry using compressed air from the surface. Then, selected bulkheads across the width of the hull were strengthened and sealed to subdivide the hull internally. Finally, by pumping in more compressed air, the great hulk was raised to the surface upside down. The work took nine months and was undertaken by thirty men. A further four capital ships comprising two battleships and two battlecruisers, together with one cruiser, were lifted by Cox and Danks Ltd. between 1927 and 1931. *Hindenburg* was the only capital ship to be raised and towed to the breakers right way up, after immense difficulties.

Metal Industries of Charlestown continued the work in 1931, employing many of Cox and Danks' workforce in otherwise difficult times. A further six capital ships were raised upside down in the same manner as that exploited by Cox, and all except the last to be lifted were towed to Rosyth for breaking.

This final ship was *Derfflinger,* a 28,000 ton battlecruiser credited with the sinking of the British battlecruisers *Queen Mary* and *Invincible* at the Battle of Jutland. *Derfflinger* was brought to the surface in 1939, and war again broke out soon after she was raised. There were now no docks available in which to dispose of her, and she remained afloat, upside down, for the duration of the Second World War. She was ultimately broken up in the Clyde in 1946.

Following the cessation of hostilities in 1945, there was a surplus of scrap metal, and no necessity to raise the remaining seven ships lying in deep water at Scapa Flow. A certain amount of salvage continued, as the ships became a prime source of low radioactive content steel, necessary for various medical and research facilities. Armour plate up to fourteen inches thick was removed from some of the battleships for this purpose.

Their ownership has since passed through a number of small salvage companies, and none of the remaining ships are now intact. The three battleships, *König, Kronprinz Wilhelm* and *Markgraf,* lie almost upside down. Their hulls have been blasted open exposing turbines and boilers from which much of the more valuable metal has been removed. The four cruisers, *Brummer, Dresden, Karlsruhe* and *Köln* lie on their sides, sections of their hulls opened to gain access to the exotic metals within their engine and boiler rooms.

In recent years, the remaining ships have become a major attraction to amateur SCUBA divers, and are regularly visited by those interested in warships, being the last accessible survivors of the mighty Dreadnought era. They remain a monument to technological achievement, and to the beginning of the end of the British Empire, which never recovered from the effects of the Great War.

Chapter 2
KÖNIG

SEINER MAJESTÄT SCHIFF *KÖNIG* was the name ship of
the fourth class of German Dreadnought battleships, successors
to the *Kaiser*-class Dreadnoughts. König herself served as
Flagship of the Third Squadron of the High Seas Fleet and under
her command were her three sister ships, *(Markgraf, Kronprinz
Wilhelm* and *Grosser Kurfürst),* and three of the *Kaiser*-class
battleships.

The *Kaiser*-class vessels — *Kaiser* herself, *Prinzregent
Luitpold, Kaiserin, König Albert* and *Friedrich der Grosse* —
were magnificent ships, but the *König*-class battleships were even
better. They were built as answer to the first of the British super-
Dreadnoughts, which had been the first battleships to carry all
their main armament along the ship's centreline, with fore and
aft turrets superimposed. This arrangement enabled all the main
guns to be fired together on a single broadside.

König had been included in the 1911 Naval Estimates of the
Reichstag, and was launched on March 1st, 1913. Following
fitting out and commissioning, she joined the High Seas Fleet on
August 10th, 1914, six days after the outbreak of war. The cost
of building *König* had been 43 million Marks, equivalent to
about £2.25 million then.

Contemporary British ships cost about £1.8 million each,
and the greater price of the German warships reflects the effort
to make them as unsinkable as possible, to withstand a British
broadside. The German designers protected the vital parts of
each ship with the thickest and densest armourplate it could
carry, and the hull was subdivided into as many watertight
compartments as possible, to restrict the effects of flooding after
holing. A compartment could be deliberately flooded to maintain

▲
SMS
König
(Author's
collection)

13

C

stability, in the case of damage to a compartment on the opposite side of the ship.

The additional subdivisions within *König* are exemplified by the nine boiler rooms used to house its fifteen boilers. The British *Orion*-class ships, with three boilers more, had only six boiler-rooms. The hull side armourplate of *König* midships was 13.75 inches thick against the 12 inches on *Orion* and the German ship had an additional torpedo bulkhead inside the hull, to absorb torpedo or mine explosions.

In all these arrangements, successful damage control was seen as a key factor for the survival of the German ships in a confrontation with the British Fleet. Compartments such as magazines could be completely flooded within 15 minutes and the German Navy regularly exercised their crews in flooding and counter-flooding exercises.

The disadvantage of some of these protective systems was the greater weight that resulted from thicker armour and additional internal pressure-resistant bulkheads. To achieve the same displacement in the water as their British counterparts, the German ships had to compensate with lighter guns, of a correspondingly smaller calibre. *König's* main armament comprised ten 12-inch guns with a range of 20,500 yards; HMS *Orion* carried the same number of 13.5-inch guns with a range of 23,100 yards, and the heavier British shells could inflict greater damage. The mastermind behind Britain's naval policy in the first decade of the century had been Lord Fisher, whose maxim was: 'Hit first and hit hard.'

The sheer size of *König* is difficult to take in from figures alone. The ship was 576 feet long — almost the length of two football pitches — and at the widest section of the hull she had a beam of 100 feet. When fully loaded with fuel and ammunition her foredeck was 22 feet above the water, her bridge 30 feet higher, and the spotting top on the foremast above the bridge was 100 feet above water level. The average modern two storey house stands at about 22 feet to the ridge tiles, so it will be appreciated what an awesome sight *König* must have made. She would have been resplendent in her pale grey livery, teak decks shining white, and black-and-white cross of the Imperial German Ensign flying at her mainmast, and the silver-and-gold crown of the King of Prussia emblazoning the *wappen* on each side of her bow.

König carried her 12-inch 50-calibre main guns in pairs on five turrets, and they were aimed from stereoscopic rangefinders on each turret and on the various control stations. The rangefinder sightings were relayed to the gunnery officer in the armoured conning tower above the bridge. There the mean of all the sightings was calculated, and the gun training angles were transmitted electrically to receiver dials within the gun houses.

On receiving signals from the gun houses that all guns were loaded and correctly aimed, the gunnery officer in the conning tower would press buttons on a panel to fire the guns electrically in any combination. The fall of shot was observed by an officer in the spotting top in the foremast high above, and his sightings reported to the conning tower for corrections of elevation and deviation to be calculated. Each gun fired a projectile weighing a little over 900 pounds which left the muzzle at a speed of about 1,750 miles per hour. These shells were stored deep down in the ship, beneath an armoured deck and behind coal bunkers and air spaces arranged in the ship's sides. The cordite propellant charges were held in the magazines, one deck below the shell rooms, and both shells and cordite charges were hoisted up the turret barbette into a working chamber below the gun house, from which they were carried up by hoists that rotated with the turret.

The shells were pushed onto loading trays and hydraulically rammed into the gun chambers when the guns were lowered to horizontal. The brass cases containing the cordite propellant were rammed home behind them. The Krupp horizontal wedge breech, also hydraulically powered, was then closed, and the gun pneumatically run out and hydraulically elevated, to be ready for firing. Each turret was provided with its own hydraulically-driven system for these functions; *König* could fire about 2½ rounds each minute from her big guns, which amounted to some feverish activity between magazines, shell rooms and turrets. A total of 84 officers and men served in the cramped working quarters of each turret and barbette, not including those locked into the shell rooms and magazines.

The ship was driven by three triple-stage Parsons turbines, the most sophisticated of the time, and also built at the Imperial Dockyard, Wilhelmshaven. Each was directly coupled to a three-bladed propeller, a little over 12½ feet in diameter, which could drive the ship to 22½ knots in extremes. The turbines were supplied with steam from the fifteen water-tube boilers with a working pressure of 227lbs per square inch, consuming coal at the rate of about 18 tons per hour. All this coal was shovelled into the furnaces by men, although the three forward boiler-rooms were totally oil-fired.

For *König* to be run as an efficient fighting ship, it was necessary for her to accommodate 1,096 officers and men, and as Flagship of the Third Battle Squadron of the High Seas Fleet, she also carried a Rear Admiral with his staff of 14 officers. In naval terms, the accommodation provided for her crew was of a high standard; the men were provided with personal lockers, and all the quarters were centrally heated by steam from the vessel's boilers. (Wartime experience, however, necessitated a substantial increase in manning levels, so that all Germany's capital ships became overcrowded and comfort was much reduced).

König's first action, although the ship fired not a single shot, was in support of the three battlecruisers, *Lützow, von der Tann* and *Moltke,* which arrived off Lowestoft early on the morning of 25th April, 1916, and in the space of ten minutes demolished 200 houses by shelling. The three ships then steamed north and repeated the exercise on Great Yarmouth. A small force of British light cruisers came on the scene and tried to delay them until the Grand Fleet could arrive, but the Germans decided on this occasion to prefer caution and retreated to their bases on the River Jade.

It was almost halfway through the war before the two Fleets met in force at the Battle of Jutland. Admiralty intelligence received reports that the German battlecruisers were about to leave port on another raid, and the British Grand Fleet put to sea on the 30th May, 1916, to carry out a sweep across the northern sector of the North Sea towards the Skagerrak.

The Battle Fleet under the command of Admiral Sir John Jellicoe set out from Scapa Flow with its 24 battleships and three battlecruisers, along with escorting destroyers and scouting cruisers. The plan was for it to rendevous off the Skagerrak with the Battlecruiser Fleet of Vice-Admiral Sir David Beatty, on his way from Rosyth with six battlecruisers, four fast battleships and attendant destroyers and scouts.

Meanwhile, the German Scouting Group of the High Seas Fleet, with five battlecruisers and their torpedo boat screen and scouting cruisers, had put to sea, and by the afternoon of 31st May, they came into contact with Beatty's ships. The two forces had been steaming on almost parallel courses, out of sight of one another over the horizon, and quite possibly might never have met, but for the chance that a Danish merchant steamer, the *N. J. Fjord,* was on route midway between them. As a neutral ship, she was stopped and given a routine search by the German torpedo boats, *B109* and *B110,* who were out on the edge of the German battlecruiser force. Meanwhile, the British light cruiser, *Galatea,* scouting on the edge of her own fleet, sighted the Danish ship and went over with the same intentions as the Germans. The *Galatea* noticed steam from the departing German torpedo boats, and they themselves saw her coming into sight and signalled their flotilla leader, SMS *Elbing.* By 15.45 in the afternoon, the two groups of battlecruisers had manoeuvred into position against each other, and furious firing commenced. A series of salvoes from *von der Tann* struck the last ship on the British battlecruiser line, HMS *Indefatigable,* which blew up in a massive explosion from her magazines.

The four fast *Queen Elizabeth*-class battleships of Beatty's force, *(Barham, Valiant, Warspite* and *Malaya),* forming the Fifth Battle Squadron, had been left some miles astern due to a signalling error, but they now started to catch up with the action, opening fire from nearly eleven miles away with their 15-inch guns. Their arrival on the scene began to redress the balance, but not before another of the six British battlecruisers, HMS *Queen Mary,* had suffered a similar fate to the *Indefatigable* from the 12-inch shells of *Derfflinger.*

By this time, however, the news came through from the cruiser, *Southampton,* scouting some miles ahead of the action, that it was not merely the German battlecruisers who were at sea. The earlier Admiralty monitoring of the German radio signals had mis-interpreted one key message, which would have told them that the force of ships putting to sea that day was in fact the full High Seas Fleet. Steaming northwards now at full speed towards the action were the six divisions of the Battle Fleet, comprising 16 Dreadnought battleships and six pre-Dreadnoughts, commanded by Vice-Admiral Scheer in the *Friedrich der Grosse* and led by Rear Admiral Paul Behncke in *König.*

This was the moment for which the British strategists had so long planned and hoped, and Beatty switched tactics to draw the German ships north towards the guns of Jellicoe's battleships, on their way from Scapa Flow. He first took his own ships south, to let the German Battle Fleet catch sight of them, and then swung back north, to run before the Germans using his superior speed. By the time the last ships in his line were altering course to turn northward, they had come into range of *König's* guns, which inflicted damage on *Malaya* and *Warspite. Malaya* took the brunt of this punishment, and many of her crew now lie buried at the Naval Cemetery at Lyness, on Hoy.

The chase north became close. The British ships had been designed to achieve speeds of up to 25 knots, but in practice barely reached 24, while the lead German ships, *König* and her sisters, were reaching speeds of up to 23 knots and maintaining a continuing fire on the British battleships. *Malaya,* despite her own casualties, managed to score some hits on *König,* causing devastation on board but failing to affect the German ship's speed or fighting power. Eventually the British drew out of range of the German guns, and now from this safe distance could continue to shell their pursuers due to the greater range of their larger armament.

The chase lasted little more than an hour, before the Germans found themselves confronted by the massed ships of Jellicoe's Battle Fleet, stretched out across the horizon in front of them to concentrate their fire on the warships entering the trap. *König* sustained further hits, some secondary armament being put out of action, and the Flagship of the German battlecruiser force, *Lützow,* already damaged in the earlier battlecruiser action, was reduced to a hulk and withdrew to sink. *17*

By this time Admiral Scheer was pulling back out of the trap, turning his whole Fleet around at once to take his line south and out of reach of the British guns. Due to the vast amount of smoke generated by the ships' boiler fires and the burning cordite from their guns, the Fleets lost sight of each other, but during this brief but furious action, *Derfflinger* found another victim when the smoke and mist lifted for a moment to reveal the luckless battlecruiser, *Invincible,* silhouetted against the northern horizon, less than 10,000 yards from her guns.

In the darkness of the smoke, Scheer turned eastwards to try to escape towards his bases, but found he was again heading towards the centre of Jellicoe's Battle Fleet, which had steamed round to cut him off. Scheer ordered his damaged battlecruisers to attack the British with no regard for the consequences, but again the guns pounded the German ships, and again *König,* still leading the German line, was hit, and this time holed. Confusion and panic broke out amongst the German Fleet, with some ships turning away without waiting for orders, causing others to stop or even go astern to avoid collisions. Admiral Behncke in *König* adroitly saved the situation by turning into the wind and creating a smokescreen to cover the German withdrawal, while German torpedo boats closed in on the British Fleet to attack the battleships, creating another smokescreen to hide their own capital ships. This action worked, with the British battleships having to take evasive measures to avoid the torpedoes, and during this time the German Fleet was lost to sight in the smoke, mist and now failing light.

König was battered but still afloat, and during the night headed for home, carrying 1,600 tons of sea water in flooded compartments, with armour plate stoved in, her foredeck and casement decks blown open, and her bows down in the water. Even when she reached the protective shelter of the German minefields, she was now drawing so much water forward that she had to wait for a high tide to clear a sandbank off the Jade to berth in Wilhelmshaven for repairs.

After two months repair work, *König* was ready to put to sea again and join other Dreadnoughts in supporting a raid by the only two serviceable battlecruisers, *Moltke* and *von der Tann.* The British had lost a greater tonnage at Jutland, (called by the Germans the Battle of Skagerrak,) but the High Seas Fleet had sustained damage to ships and to morale from the pounding of the British guns. Scheer's answer was to plan a raid on Sunderland on 19th August, 1916, again trying to draw out a section of the Grand Fleet to combat on unequal terms.

Again Admiralty intelligence brought the British Fleet out in readiness, but scouting Zeppelins led Scheer to alter direction, through the incorrect information that a division of unrelated British cruisers and destroyers were in fact an exposed detachment of British battleships from the Grand Fleet. The move took him off course from an encounter with Jellicoe's actual ships, and by the time he realised his mistake a German U-boat sighted the Grand Fleet and warned him of the danger. Scheer headed for home and avoided what could have been a fatal confrontation. For a time afterwards *König* lay idle at the German Naval base at Wilhelmshaven, apart from visits to Kiel for gunnery and training exercises in the Baltic. (The British Fleet had now gained four battleships and five battlecruisers against Germany's two additional battleships, and German Naval strategy and shipbuilding was aimed at strangling Britain by destroying her merchant fleet through U-boat warfare).

By 1917, the successful uprising in Russia had added to feelings of discontent shown by German Naval crews, following a harsh winter, poor harvests and deteriorating rations for all but the officers. Hunger strikes and harsh punishments culminated on 25th July in the murder at Wilhelmshaven of the commanding officer of the *König Albert,* and the shooting of the leaders of the mutiny. *König* and the ships of the 5th Division were not as seriously affected by this unrest, and took part in an operation in October, 1917, to back units of German infantry invading the Baltic islands of Oesel, Dagoe and Moon. Shooting accurately at maximum range, *König* fatally crippled the Russian battleship *Slava,* the last time her own guns were fired in battle.

König's final voyage was to meet up again with the British Fleet to enter internment in Scapa Flow. She was unable to raise steam for the voyage at this time, as due to inactivity and lack of maintenance some condenser tubes were leaking. Following re-tubing, *König* joined her sisters in Scapa Flow on 6th December, 1918.

Diving on KÖNIG

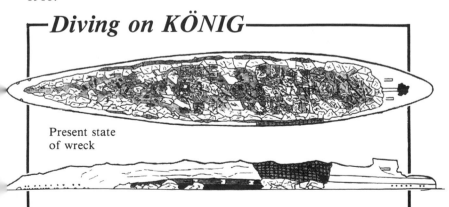

Present state
of wreck

On 21st June, 1919, König disappeared beneath the surface of Scapa Flow in position **N 58° 52' 14"**, **W 03° 09' 07"** capsizing to port as she sank. Loose items on deck — hatch

covers, ventilator cowls and abandoned rigging screws —
hurtled across her vast empty decks as she turned. Air
erupted from open doors beneath the surface making the
water boil above, as compartments 90 feet below the
surface were crushed by weight of water, and the trapped
air within was released to find its way up through the ship
and out.

She settled on the bottom of Scapa Flow, her masts
broken, port side down, her funnels and bridge crushed but
resting on the thick clay beneath the light surface silt. As
the years passed, the massive weight of her hull forced her
superstructure deeper into the clay, and today the ship lies
almost upside down, although gaps can be found still
between her starboard decks and the seabed. She lies with
her bows pointing approximately south-east, in 34-37
metres of water depending on the tide, and is now the most
damaged of the German ships lying in the Flow.

She was untouched by Cox and Danks and also by
Metal Industries, who decided that other ships presented
less problems in being raised. During the 1960s and 1970s,
however, Nundy Metals used SCUBA divers to place
charges on her hull plates to tear them open. The wreck
was progressively blasted and her inside torn out.
Armourplate was removed as were hull plates, so some side
sections of the ship are removed as far in as the inner
protective bulkhead, leaving the outer frames protruding
like ribs on a carcase. Her bow frames and hull plates are
collapsed, spread across the seabed, and the bow is only
recognisable by the massive anchor hawse pipes, like eyes
staring unblinkingly at the passing diver.

From the forward-pointing torpedo tube in the bow,
aft to the centre propeller shaft housing, the vessel's hull is
opened up, exposing the tangled remains of shell racks,
boiler casings and firebars, generators and turbines. Finning
further aft, more shell racks and steam pipes are passed
until the port rudder is seen ahead, still supported on its
pivot. The stern is virtually intact from the rudder aft, but
partly buried into the seabed.

Finning forward again, on the seabed and along the
starboard side, the diver passes slabs of armourplate broken
from its mounting bolts which have eroded away, the
plating having fallen to the seabed to sink slowly into the
soft clay. Behind this, and the wreckage of a funnel, the
diver can pass under the forecastle deck, still remarkably
clean and intact, as the only light penetrating under the
hull is that from the diver's torch and so there is no marine

growth to cover the teak deck planking.

Almost on hands and knees, and finning further beneath the upturned hull, the diver finally arrives at the side of the centre turret of *König*. There is only about four feet between seabed and deck at this point, the turret being more than half buried in the bottom of Scapa Flow; the guns themselves are hidden from view, covered by soft silt formed on the seabed.

A hole can be found in the gun house floor, through which the empty brass cordite cases were thrown at Jutland after their contents had driven the shells out of the gun barrels and on their way to HMS *Malaya*. Shining the torch through this hole and into the upturned gun house, shell-handling racks can be seen amongst the debris below, which covers the breech end of the awesome starboard gun. The seabed has not yet encroached inside, but time passes too quickly and the diver has to grope his way back through the stirred sediment, which reduces the visibility to zero, to escape the oppressiveness beneath the hull and go back up into the green light filtering through the water from above.

Passing a 5.9-inch casemate gun, secondary armament of the ship and used to fend off attacking British destroyers, and passing too a winch, still with rope wound on the barrel, the diver fins from beneath the deck and up the hull side to arrive at the starboard bilge keel, beyond which the hull is opened. He now has to leave the sleeping giant to regain the surface, where the glare of the Orkney sun can take him momentarily by surprise, while the congers and wrasse settle down to their peaceful existence in Admiral Behncke's former Flagship.

KÖNIG-CLASS BATTLESHIP

(This layout applies to KÖNIG, MARKGRAF and KRONPRINZ WILHELM)

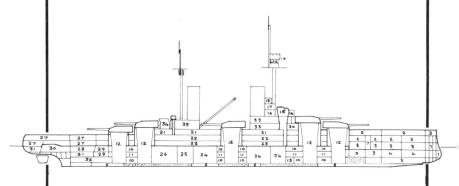

1 Bow frames and air spaces
2 Crew spaces
3 Stores
4 Trimming tanks
5 Bow torpedo room
6 Double bottom: shaded area = oil storage
7 Cable lockers
8 Capstan machinery
9 Forward beam torpedo room
10 Shell rooms
11 Magazines
12 12-inch turret barbettes
13 Forward lower control room
14 Compass platform
15 Conning tower

16 Chart house
17 Captain's day cabin
18 Admiral's day cabin
19 Spotting top
20 Radio rooms, damage control centres, drying rooms
21 150 mm gun casemates
22 Crew messes, galleys, bakery, offices and drying rooms
23 Engineers and stokers wash-rooms, engineers stores, workshops, boiler room induction fans

24 Boiler rooms
25 HP turbine room
26 LP turbine room
27 Officers accom.
28 Emerg. steering compartment
29 After beam torpedo room
30 Rudder machinery
31 Trimming tanks
32 Shaft tunnel
33 Boiler room forced draught intakes
34 Turbine room ventilation

Chapter 3
KRONPRINZ WILHELM

INCLUDED in the Naval Estimates of 1912 and laid down in
the summer months of that year, this ship, (originally named
simply *Kronprinz),* was the last of the *König*-class Dreadnoughts
to be completed. She was built at the Krupp's Germania shipyard
at Kiel; builders of many of the vessels of the High Seas Fleet
and one of Germany's most prolific shipyards. The vessel was
launched on 21st February, 1914, and after fitting out and trials,
she joined the Third Battle Squadron of the High Seas Fleet in
January, 1915. This coincided with the promotion to
Commander of Squadron III of Admiral Reinhard Scheer, (soon
to be promoted again to Commander-in-Chief of the High Seas
Fleet).

   Kronprinz was almost identical to *König,* but in the absence
of Rear Admiral's accommodation, the superstructure between
forefunnel and bridge was less cluttered, and she was built with a
heavy foremast, not fitted to her sisters until later.

   In addition to their main armament of ten 12-inch guns, the
Königs mounted fourteen 5.9-inch guns on the battery deck, each
housed singly on its own rotating pedestal with the barrels
protruding from hull sides. Each of these guns was protected by
a 6.75-inch thick steel turret front which rotated with the gun.
Of 50 calibres, the barrels were 24′ 6″ long and weighed a little
over 5½ tons. The total weight of the complete gun mounting
was over 14 tons, and they were capable of firing a 101 lb shell
an effective distance of over eight miles, seven times per minute.
These guns were used to engage attacking small craft such as
destroyers, which would be attempting to fire their torpedoes at
the broad sides of the battleships. Little wonder that few of these
mighty ships, British or German, were struck by torpedos from

▲
SMS
*Kronprinz
Wilhelm*
(Author's
collection)

23

destroyers. (At the Battle of Jutland, however, no fewer than 13 destroyers and torpedo boats succumbed to such hails of gunfire from battleships and battlecruisers). These principally defensive guns could be aimed from the control tower above the bridge in a similar manner to the ship's main armament, but could only be fired at the gun. In the event of the aiming positions being struck by shells and knocked out in battle, the gun crews each had their own telescopic sights.

Kronprinz and her sisters also carried six 3.4-inch guns, three each side of her forward superstructure below the bridge. They could fire a 20lb shell a similar distance to the 5.9-inch guns. Two further 3.4-inch guns on the superstructure aft of the after funnel could be elevated to 80 degrees to engage aircraft or airships. (In the Second World War, battleships bristled with anti-aircraft armament of all kinds).

Magazines of the *König*-class ships were air-conditioned to stabilise the temperature of the cordite shell propellant. Cordite could increase its temperature under certain conditions, and a number of ships were lost when such cordite spontaneously ignited. (Probably the most famous was the British Dreadnought battleship, *Vanguard,* of 1910, which disintegrated while at anchor in Scapa Flow on 9th July, 1917).

Kronprinz and her sisters were constructed with five deck levels within the hull. Below the casemate deck was the middle deck. This contained crews' mess spaces, offices, drying rooms and locker rooms. Below this was the armoured deck, the thickness of which varied from 62mm to 120mm as protection for the ship's vital parts and upon which were coal bunkers, store rooms and engineers' workshops. Beneath the armoured deck, just below the waterline, lay the upper platform deck. It did not run the full length of the ship, being interrupted in places by large machinery such as boilers and turbines from the deck below, carrying the twenty shell rooms, the anchor capstan motors and machinery forward, and aft the steering gear for the twin rudders. The lower platform deck was below, again interrupted by large machinery. It housed the magazines containing the cordite shell propellant, four torpedo rooms to supply and operate the underwater beam torpedo tubes, fresh water tanks and storerooms. The turbines, boilers, propeller shaft-bearing pedestals and gyro compass rooms and the forward torpedo room in the bow were yet another deck down. Beneath this was the ship's double bottom containing spaces for fresh water and oil.

Crew accommodation on the middle deck was directly below the 5.9-inch casemate gun emplacements, abeam of boiler flue and ventilator ducting arranged fore and aft along the ship's centreline. These areas were centrally heated from the ship's boilers. The temperature was maintained at 50 degrees Fahrenheit, (a luxury not afforded to sailors of other countries' navies until the next generation of battleships). Officers' accommodation was mostly aft, beneath the quarter-deck and on two levels. The ship's Captain and other senior officers had additional cabins on and below the bridge. Officers had their own cabins, (but shared from the rank of Sub-Lieutenant down). The accommodation, which included bathrooms and offices, was centrally heated to about 58 degrees Fahrenheit.

The *Königs* were fitted with emergency control stations from where they could be steered and commanded. One was on the upper platform deck directly below the forward conning tower and connected to it through an armoured vertical trunking; another was below the after conning tower. Forward, the ships were taken up variously with anchor chain lockers, storerooms, water tanks and further crew spaces.

The navigation instruments typified the advanced technology throughout, having 2 gyro compasses with repeaters in all the control positions to facilitate accurate position fixing, and depth finders. A labyrinth of voice pipes was the principal method of communication between varous departments, but telephones were provided between some areas.

On joining the Fleet, *Kronprinz* made up the full complement of battleships of the Third Squadron, which had never carried out exercises with all the ships together. Admiral Scheer immediately applied to take his squadron to the Baltic by way of the Kiel Canal for exercises. Such training could not be carried out off Germany's North Sea bases owing to the presence of British minefields and submarines, but the Germans had the advantage of access to the safer waters of the Baltic. (The relative limitations of Scapa Flow for exercises was a principal reason for the superior gunnery shown by the German ships in battle). Before the exercises, however, a foray against Britain's east coast cities was planned. During January of 1915, a succession of gales kept the German Fleet in port, and when the winds finally subsided, German minesweepers found that vast new fields had been laid down by the enterprising British during the bad weather. The plan was finally abandoned.

The following month, the Commander-in-Chief of the High Seas Fleet, Admiral von Ingenohl, was replaced by the former Chief of the Naval Staff, Admiral von Pohl. He was expected to achieve results which would deplete the numbers of the steadily growing British Grand Fleet. In an attempt to do so, the main units of the German Fleet were to be sent out to entice the British onto carefully prepared minefields. This plan failed. Bad weather during much of 1915 prevented most sorties from being undertaken, and Jellicoe was not one to risk the British Fleet so recklessly. The successes of the German Armies on the Eastern Front demanded the detachment of some naval units to the

Baltic to protect German Divisions from sea-borne attack from the Russian Navy. Squadron III was moved from Wilhelmshaven to Cuxhaven on the Elbe, from where they could quickly pass through the Kiel Canal if required.

By September, 1915, Squadron III was back at Wilhelmshaven having seen no action. The ships were taken out of service for the fitting of new rangefinders and renewal of their propeller shaft aftermost bearings. *Kronprinz* and her sisters rejoined the Fleet in October, when a further sortie to entice the Grand Fleet out was abandoned. In Feburary, 1916, Admiral von Pohl died and was succeeded by Admiral Scheer — a more aggressive personality who had far greater ambitions for the German Navy than either of his predecessors. His arguments persuaded the Kaiser to allow Scheer to use his ships in a more offensive manner.

The German Commander-in-Chief could not risk a battle against the numerically superior British Grand Fleet. Their five *Queen Elizabeths* and the soon-to-be commissioned five *Revenge*-class Dreadnoughts he knew to be superior fighting ships to any in the German Fleet. Scheer therefore planned to continue with further battlecruiser raids on British east coat cities to draw out detachments of the Grand Fleet towards hidden U-boats and battleships.

The first venture planned was an attack on British destroyers and light cruisers. They were continuously patrolling the southwestern area of the North Sea, (known to the Germans as the Hoofden), searching for enterprising U-boats and ensuring that neutral merchant shipping was not carrying goods for Germany. Early on the morning of March 5th, 1916, the German ships left their bases, the battlecruisers supported by the battleships, including *Kronprinz*. In the Hoofden, only the periscopes of British submarines were reported. Not prepared to lose any of his ships to torpedo attacks, Scheer instructed the Fleet to withdraw back to their bases with nothing accomplished except manoeuvring practice. On 25th April, *Kronprinz* was one of the battleships of Squadron III supporting the raid by the battlecruisers on Yarmouth and Lowestoft, when none of the battleships was obliged to use their guns.

At the Battle of Jutland, on the 31st May, 1916, *Kronprinz* was the fourth ship in the line of battleships behind *König*. Joining in the chase northwards of the British battlecruisers and the *Queen Elizabeth* battleships of the Fifth Division, she opened fire on the last in line, HMS *Malaya*. As the British drew away from their tormentors, *Kronprinz* was the last to lose range on them. Then the *König*-class battleships in the van of the German line were suddenly faced by the 24 Dreadnought battleships of the British Battle Fleet. British fire commenced immediately the German ships were sighted. The Germans, however, were unable to distinguish the enemy units through the smoke and gunfire from the numerous smaller actions taking place on the vast expanse of sea separating the two Battle Fleets. They soon discerned, however, the orange flashes of the British big guns, stretching from west to east as far as could be seen. Nerves of iron were now required by the crews on the German battleships as they waited for the onslaught of the British shells.

Kronprinz was a lucky ship that day; she suffered not a single hit as her guns ranged with difficulty on the gun flashes almost seven miles away. When Scheer pressed for home that night, he left behind two sunk cruisers, three torpedo boats and the sinking battlecruiser, *Lützow.* He was yet to lose a battleship, two more cruisers and a further two torpedo boats during the night, but *Kronprinz* arrived back at Wilhelmshaven on June 1st, unscathed and with no casualties.

Kronprinz was next involved in the raid on Sunderland on August 13th, 1916, when Scheer's ships narrowly escaped the massed guns of the British Fleet. Then, she took part in a movement out into the open waters of the North Sea, in yet another failed attempt to draw the British towards waiting U-boats.

On November 17th, 1916, the ships of Squadron III were despatched to cover torpedo boat flotillas and tugs during an attempt to recover the U-boat, *U-20,* (which, a year before, had sunk the Cunard liner, *Lusitania),* stranded together with *U-30,* on a sandbank off the west coast of Denmark. The rescue failed and *U-20* had to be demolished by explosive charges where she lay. (*U-30* had extricated herself before the rescue ships arrived). As the big ships patrolled further out to sea to protect the rescue operations, they were spotted by the British submarine, *J1,* and both *Kronprinz* and *Grosser Kurfürst* were torpedoed. *Kronprinz* was holed abeam of the bridge, but saved from extensive damage by her substantial inboard protection.

After repairs, *Kronprinz* lapsed into inactivity during the winter of 1916-17, when much of Scheer's time was taken up with arguing for the resumption of unrestricted U-boat warfare against commercial shipping supplying Britain. He was correctly convinced that this was the quickest way to defeat Germany's principal enemy. In February 1917, the Reichstag finally agreed to allow his U-boats to sink merchant ships without warning. In consequence, Scheer now had to transfer some of his more experienced officers from the capital ships to crew the increasing number of U-boats. These officers were replaced by inexperienced men who were less able to deal with the crews under them.

By this time the German Fleet had been strengthened by the new battleships *Baden* and *Bayern,* and Scheer moved his flag to *Baden,* adding *Bayern* to Squadron III. This re-organisation demanded Fleet manoeuvres, and during such movements in the

Heligoland Bight, on March 5th, 1917, *Kronprinz* and *Grosser Kurfürst* collided at high speed, both ships suffering extensive damage. With two such vital ships out of commission for some weeks, the Fleet lay idle, Scheer being unable to risk battle. The big ships were not called to action until October, by which time the first signs of discontent amongst the crews of the battleships of Squadron IV had erupted, and been quelled.

The ships of Squadron III, including *Kronprinz,* were called upon to support the landing of infantry divisions on the Baltic islands of Oesel, Dagoe and Moon in the Gulf of Riga. They were held by the Russians and used as a base for their Fleet, which posed a threat to the German Army divisions occupying the city of Riga on the eastern Baltic shores. Learning from the mistakes made by the Allied forces in Gallipoli in 1915, the Germans sent 10 Dreadnought battleships, a battlecruiser, 6 cruisers and 50 torpedo boats to support landings by 25,000 troops facing puny opposition. The success of the operation raised morale within the Navy, and the action was a welcome relief from boredom for the ships' crews.

On the 27th January, 1918, Kaiser Wilhelm II's 59th birthday, *Kronprinz* was renamed *Kronprinz Wilhelm* in his honour. She was the only ship of the *König* class to be given such personalisation, her sisters all retaining simple German titles.

The last operation by the German Fleet was to attack merchant shipping en route between Britain and Norway. Britain had strengthened convoy escorts after successful German attacks, and Scheer's response was to send battlecruisers and battleships to attack instead of light forces. Accordingly, on April 23rd, 1918, the battlecruisers made their way out to sea, followed by all Germany's battleships including *Kronprinz Wilhelm.* At 6.00 a.m. the following morning, a signal was received by Scheer that the battlecruiser *Moltke* had lost her inner starboard propeller, resulting in the driving turbine overspeeding and the disintegration of a cast gear wheel. Pieces of this had penetrated condensers, steam pipes and the deck head to the switchboard rooms. Flooding followed, eventually causing the boilers to block up. The ship was virtually crippled, and the ensuing masses of radio messages were quickly intercepted by British intelligence. Thirty one battle ships of the Grand Fleet left their bases, but the Germans reached the safety of their own minefields before the British found them.

Kronprinz Wilhelm now lay idle at Wilhelmshaven until sent to Kiel on November 1st in an attempt to isolate revolutionary elements. Insubordination raged amongst the crew members as she arrived at Kiel. High Command believed the mutinous elements could be brought to order, thinking the sailors based at the Wik Barracks ashore were loyal to them. Marines sent to arrest groups of sailors, however, joined them instead, and total disorder reigned. The Fleet, and the War, were finished. On November 4th, *Kronprinz Wilhelm* was put to sea by loyal crew members to prevent her from being boarded by revolutionaries and her guns from being used against loyal establishments ashore. She returned for disarmament when the terms for internment were concluded, when uncontrollable hordes looted the ship: binoculars, telescopes, ropes, paint and crockery were taken ashore to be exchanged for drink and various other pleasures, while loyal sailors toiled to empty shell rooms and magazines.

Finally, on November 27th, 1918, having left behind a chaotic Germany, *Kronprinz Wilhelm* arrived at Scapa Flow, where she lay in disrepair for seven months. The ship went to her grave at 13.15 on June 21st, 1919. Patches of oil, floating debris and occasional gushes of air marked her final resting place for several hours after she turned over to starboard in her final plunge.

Diving on KRONPRINZ WILHELM

Kronprinz Wilhelm now lies in position **N 58° 53′ 39″**, **W 03° 09′ 48″**, her starboard decks embedded in the silt and shale of the seabed in up to 38 metres of water (depending on the tide), and port side deck some distance clear of the bottom. A 5.9-inch casemate gun barrel hangs pointing down to the seabed, forced beyond maximum elevation by the weight of fallen armour plate from the hull side above, the barrel in turn forcing off the turret top. Finning forward at casemate deck level and behind fallen hull plating, the diver passes each of these secondary armament guns, one broken from its mounting. The turret lies upside down on the seabed, the pedestal torn from its fixings by a combination of sheer weight and weakening due to salvors' work higher up in the hull. Jammed beneath this gun, inaccessible due to fallen steel plating, lies the ship's fog horn, miraculously intact, surrounded by bent and buckled plates, some of which must have been the ship's forefunnel. A little forward of this is the tubular foremast, lying flat on the seabed. Looking along — as if up the mast — the diver sees the broken remains of the lower platform, which was the 5.9-inch gun control station. Immediately beyond, the spotting top lies on its side on the seabed. The top lies just off and the interior is empty of everything save hanging electric cables and switches. The diver fins back to the hull of the wreck, soon arriving forward of the mast where the hull is blasted open. Twisted hull frames lie in confusion with pipework, heavy electric cables, switchboxes and broken pump castings.

Much further aft along the wreck, beneath the overhanging deck, is the after superimposed 12-inch gun turret. The top is embedded in the seabed, with the underside of the half-buried barrels still visible. Finning up the turret front, the top of the barbette is in the superstructure deck, and aft is the top of the aftermost 12-inch turret. Checking the soundness of the quarterdeck above, the diver moves along the turret side to the front, and round to the port barrel. Moving gently along the barrel to avoid stirring sediment, the diver passes the first 'step' at the termination of the outer jacket, and then the second before arriving at the muzzle, some 35 feet from the front of the turret. The end of the barrel is jammed into the teak still covering the quarterdeck, which is noted to be buckled down towards the seabed. As the diver turns to face the open muzzle of this massive gun, to the left in the torchlight is the starboard gun in a similar position. Following the port barrel back to the turret, the diver emerges from the quarterdeck, having located guns of the ship's main armament. (This pair are the only accessible survivors of all the guns fired by the main armament of the capital ships on either side at Jutland).

Having emerged from beneath the decks of *Kronprinz Wilhelm,* the diver fins aft and approaches the stern. Entering a large hole in the port side, torchlight picks out corroded pans and shards of crockery in the remains of a galley. Above and on top of the stern, the rudders still stand intact, and further forward the propeller shaft and bearing pedestals stand clear of the bottom plating. Forward along the starboard side, plating has been removed, opening up vast, empty dark spaces; voids which were the protective spaces arranged along the hull sides. Sections of the bottom of the ship's hull have been removed to expose turbine blades within shattered casings, and twisted, distorted boiler tubes. Nevertheless, *Kronprinz Wilhelm* remains easily identifiable as one of the finest examples of fighting ship technology from the days of the mighty Dreadnought battleship era.

Chapter 4
MARKGRAF

INCLUDED in the Naval Estimates of 1911, *Markgraf* was launched at Bremen on 4th June, 1913, and joined the Fleet twelve months later. She was the third of the *König*-class Dreadnoughts to be completed and was almost identical to *König,* but without the Vice Admiral's accommodation aft of the bridge. Although a fine addition to the High Seas Fleet, the cost of building such ships was becoming an embarassment to the German treasury. For *Markgraf* alone the costs were about £2.5 million (£1.5m for hull and machinery, £900,000 for armament and £70,000 for torpedo equipment) — the equivalent of thousands of millions at today's rates. In 1913, it is claimed that Germany spent a staggering 90% of her income on defence. Certainly, after the *König*-class ships were completed, capital ship building was much reduced in Germany.

Several alterations were made to *Markgraf* and her sisters during the war. After the Battle of Jutland, the anti-torpedo nets, (suspended outboard of the ship's sides from timber booms hinged from the hull,) were totally discarded. For these to be effective necessitated a maximum speed of only eight knots — too slow to be of any value in battle. When not in use, the heavy nets were stowed on platforms projecting along the ship's sides on the casemate deck level. At Jutland, some ships received hits there and the trailing remains of the nets threatened to tangle in propellers.

During the October 1916 refit, *Markgraf* was fitted with a heavy tubular foremast in place of the slender pole type mast originally installed. The replacement was a more stable base for the new stereoscopic long base rangefinder fitted to the spotting top, from which the ship's gunnery offier could read the target's

▲
SMS
Markgraf
(Imperial
War
Museum)

32

range. The accurate aiming of a ship's guns had become a complex science by the outbreak of the Great War, when battle ranges had increased to as far as 10 miles and the flight time of a shell could be half a minute. The collation of much information was necessary before the guns could be aimed. The deflection caused by the prevailing wind had to be allowed for; similarly, the effect to the shell's flight of the forward momentum of the firing ship and its roll and pitch. Rifling or grooving in the gun barrel (to ensure the shell flew nose first) imparted a spinning momentum on the shell, which in turn caused it to drift off a straight line. Wear in a gun barrel also affected the accuracy of the shell. Finally, corrections had to be made for the angle of bearing between the ship's rangefinder and a gun turret 200 feet aft of the rangefinder. The answers to some problems were known before a ship was taken into action, but many other factors had to be calculated quickly and precisely on the spot. The German Dreadnoughts carried stereoscopic rangefinders in each big gun turret, in which two lenses, mounted 3 metres apart, were focused until the target image was in line with a cross in the rangefinder eyepiece. At this point the range could be read off a scale, and the gunlayer could elevate his guns accordingly.

The training of the guns was directed from the main Control Tower mounted above the Compass Platform on the *Königs*. The information from the various rangefinders was passed to the Gunnery Control where the mean of the readings was fed into a device called a range/deflection reporter, comprising a series of graduated slides all interlinked through rods and pivots. Each slide was set to the correct calibration, which was continuously up-dated. Thus, the rate of change of range and bearing of the target could be predicted off another scale on the instrument. The guns could be thus trained and elevated to the correct angles to allow for both the target's and the attacking ship's movements. After firing, the fall of shot was observed from the spotting top and reported to the control position as over, under or straddle, and any corrections necessary could be fed into the range/deflector. Once the range had been found, salvoes would be fired from one gun of each turret alternately, to maintain a rapid firing rate of about 25 shells per minute.

Late in 1916, the six 3.4-inch guns beneath the bridge were removed and the spaces used for additional accommodation, wireless telegraphy rooms and damage control centre. Two further high angle 3.4-inch guns were added on the aft superstructure, beneath, but outboard of, the searchlight platforms.

The *König*-class ships were fitted with five underwater torpedo tubes, each launching 50cm torpedoes which carried 250 kg of high explosive. They were powered by compressed air and

guided by gyro compass. The launching tubes could be angled
through 90 degrees, and the torpedoes were aimed through
rangefinders fitted on the casemate deckhead between numbers 4
and 5 casemate guns. This sophisticated armament, however, was
only used successfully in training exercises. Jealous of their
technology, all the rangefinders and associated instruments were
removed from their capital ships by the Germans prior to
internment.

The ships carried 5 motor-powered boats from 8·5-14·5
metres long, one 10-metre steam boat and 5 unpowered boats
6-11 metres long. These were carried on trolleys along rails to be
stowed out of the way, and winches were mounted on the decks
for pulling the boat trolleys to and from their stowage spaces.
The boats were lifted into and out of the water by the two 10-ton
hydraulic cranes which were such a distinctive feature of the
ships.

The massive searchlights were another distinctive feature,
and the Germans were well-practised in night battle tactics. The
searchlights, powered by carbon arc, would initially send out a
small beam of light while the guns were aimed. Then they would
be fully opened to dazzle the enemy who would be immediately
blasted by a salvo of 12-inch shells. During the night following
the Battle of Jutland, two British cruisers succumbed to this
clever use of lights.

The water tube boilers fitted to the ships were the ultimate
in boiler design of the time, but the boiler tubes suffered
considerably from the corrosive waste gases produced by poor
quality coal burnt by the German ships. This necessitated the
frequent, arduous work of re-tubing. The three forward boilers
were solely oil-fired, whereas coal-burning British ships of the
era were fitted with supplementary oil burners for the ships to
achieve maximum speeds.

Propulsion was by three triple stage Parsons turbines — a
British invention first adopted by the German Navy following a
visit to Britain by German technical experts in 1903. Brown
Boveri of Germany built them and they were first introduced
into the battlecruiser *von der Tann* of 1910, but not fitted to
German battleships until the *Kaiser*-class of 1912.

Markgraf and her class were reputed to be good sea-keeping
vessels, stable in rough weather with a slow but gentle roll and
pitch, and heeling only 8 degrees when turning on full rudder.

Sixteen watertight bulkheads divided the ships transversely
into seventeen main compartments, each of which was subdivided
to form a honeycomb within the hull. The armour plate was a
low carbon nickel alloy steel called Ridel steel, each plate having
been surface hardened by heat treatment following manufacture.
(Purely as an experiment, the author attempted to put a saw cut
in a piece of armour plate on *Markgraf,* and quickly blunted the

saw blade while the steel remained untouched!)

During the war, *Markgraf* was involved in the same manoeuvres and sorties as her sister ships prior to the Battle of Jutland. At that skirmish she was third ship in line in the German Battle Fleet, under the command of one Kapitän Seiferling. Joining battle for the northwards chase, *Markgraf* fired her guns for the first time in anger, probably aiming them at HMS *Malaya*. However, during this phase of the battle, *Markgraf* was herself hit by three 15-inch shells from either *Warspite* or *Malaya*. The first and second hits did not explode, but caused damage to the mast of the starboard crane and the foremast. The third shell struck the hull side armour plate on the waterline aft of the aftermost 12-inch gun turret, holing the 8-inch armour and tearing open hull seams, causing flooding in some officers' accommodation areas. The fighting efficiency of the ship was unimpaired, and just before the British battleships joined the action, *Markgraf* contributed to the sinking of the British cruiser *Defence*.

On the initial meeting of the opposing Battle Fleets, the ships of the German Squadron III were fired upon by the *Orion*-class battleships of the British First Battle Squadron: (*Orion* herself, *Monarch, Conqueror* and *Thunderer*). As they deployed to form a single line of ships ahead of the Germans, *Markgraf* was hit again, this time by a 13·5-inch shell. It detonated on the casemate side armour, adjacent to number 6 port casemate 5.9-inch gun, holing the armour and killing all but two of the gun crew. Another shell bent the port propeller shaft which necessitated shutting down the port turbine and thus losing speed.

Markgraf maintained her place in line as the Germans turned away from the British to head east. After their second turn, which brought them into the British line again, the ships of the Third Squadron came under heavy fire as they tried to extricate themselves. *Markgraf* was to some extent shielded by the two leading ships, but she received another hit from the fourteen 12-inch guns of the battleship *Agincourt*. It struck the hull forward, on the 200mm armour plate on the port side, forward of the foremost casemate gun. The torpedo net platform above was damaged and the booms shattered. The net hung from the stowage platform and some compartments within the ship flooded as a result of this hit.

In another sphere of the battle, the British light cruiser *Calliope* was drawn onto the 5·9-inch guns of *Markgraf* as the Germans were forming into line to steam home. *Markgraf* damaged two of the British cruiser's 6-inch guns, but received a hit at the base of her forefunnel, causing boiler smoke to be emitted in profusion from the severed flue pipes. She used her guns for the last time at the Battle of Jutland during the early hours of the 1st June, opening fire on dimly discernible British destroyers, but without effect. Of the German Battleships, *Markgraf* had fired the most salvoes from her 12-inch main armament, probably with considerable success. On arrival back in Germany, she was docked and repaired in Hamburg, and rejoined Squadron III on the 20th July, 1916.

With the other ships of Squadron III, *Markgraf* was included in the two futile sorties in August and October, 1916. She was also a unit of the Fleet during the final sortie, when the plan to intercept Allied convoys off Norway was called off after the battlecruiser *Moltke* became disabled.

During the spring and summer of 1918, *Markgraf* lay idle at her berth in Wilhelmshaven with the rest of the Fleet. Then, as the Allies developed more effective measures against U-boats, the German Admiralty began drafting reluctant sailors from the capital ships to serve on the U-boats. This created another blow to morale for those seamen unwilling to chance their luck in the undersea service.

On August 2nd, 1917, 600 of the crew of the *Kaiser*-class Dreadnought, *Prinzregent Luitpold* walked off the ship at Wilhelmshaven. This was in protest against the arrest of eleven of her crew — the culmination of a series of events stemming from a protest about the quality of rations. On most of the big ships, the men were harshly treated by their officers, those on *Prinzregent Luitpold* being amongst the most hated in the Fleet, and the most unbending.

While the 600 rebels were ashore, the officers raided their lockers. They found pamphlets and the names of the leaders of each ship's 'Central Committee', (formed on all the capital ships during the summer to demand an improvement in the standard of victualling.) Arrangements for a meeting the following day of each ship's committees were also found. When the 600 crew members of the *Prinzregent Luitpold* returned peacefully to their ship in the early evening, the ship was immediately moved to anchor in isolation in Schillig Roads off Wilhelmshaven.

On the 3rd August, the Committee meeting was stormed by the Wilhelmshaven police. Sixty men were arrested and there was uproar amongst the ships' crews, taking the authorities by surprise. The German Admiralty capitulated and agreed to improve rations, and the rebel leaders were now abandoned by their followers to their fate. On August 5th, the ships were taken out to sea for exercises to keep the minds of the men occupied.

Following the trial of the sixty ringleaders, those least involved were sentenced to 90 days detention, followed by an unenviable detachment in the Naval Brigade fighting on the Flanders front. Others were sentenced to terms of imprisonment ranging from seven to ten years, and the five main troublemakers were sentenced to death. Admiral Scheer, with whom the final

Decklight on
foredeck of
◀ SMS *Köln*

Bridge support
steelwork and
scuttle in watch
officers cabin,
SMS *Brummer* ▶

No. 1 port 6 inch
casemate gun,
HMS *Royal Oak* ▼

Plumose anemone ▲

Port anchor capstan
and chain, foredeck,
◄ SMS *Brummer*

▲ Cuckoo Wrasse

Starboard propeller
shaft end bearing
bracket, *V83* ▶

Plumose anemone ▼

Inside spotting top,
instruments removed
leaving plugs hanging
on flexible conduit,
SMS *Markgraf* ▶

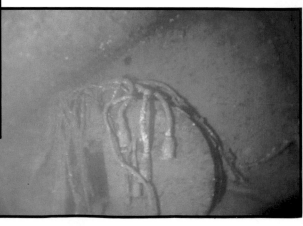

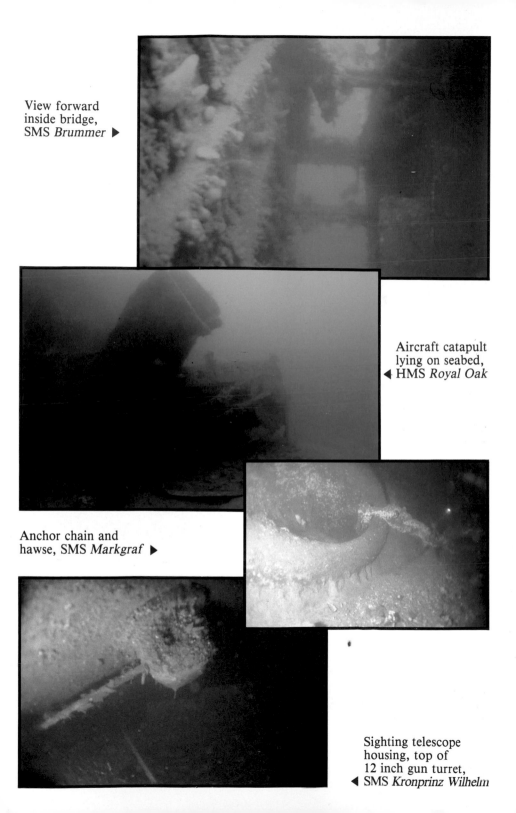

View forward inside bridge, SMS *Brummer* ▶

Aircraft catapult lying on seabed, ◀ HMS *Royal Oak*

Anchor chain and hawse, SMS *Markgraf* ▶

Sighting telescope housing, top of 12 inch gun turret, ◀ SMS *Kronprinz Wilhelm*

0.5 inch quadruple
machine guns,
HMS *Royal Oak* ▼

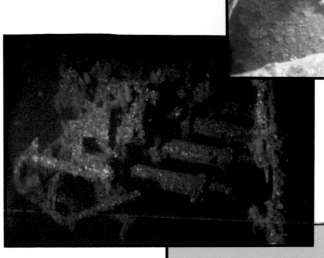

Porthole on wrecked
▲ stern of *F2*

Anchor capstan drive
clutch, site of
SMS *Bremse* ▶

Dahlia anemone ▼

No. 2 starboard
150mm casemate gun,
viewed from forward,
SMS *Markgraf* ▶

decision rested, commuted this to 15 years imprisonment for three of the men. As an example, however, he confirmed the death penalty on stokers Reichpietsch and Kobis, who had attempted to gain the support of a left-wing minority party in the Reichstag. At dawn on September 5th, at a Military establishment in Cologne, they were executed by firing squad.

After the invasion of the Baltic islands in October 1917, the big ships again became idle. U-boat losses increased, and on land the German armies began to lose ground. On October 18th, 1918, Admiral von Hipper, (who had succeeded Scheer as Commander-in-Chief), assembled the massed German Fleet in Schillig Roads planning a last attempt to do battle with British detachments. The German ships were aflame with rumour that this was to be a final suicide mission to redeem the name of the German High Seas Fleet. The crew of *Markgraf* erupted into riot, the noise carried over to those in the other ships, and crew members of the Dreadnought *Thuringen* barricaded themselves in the forecastle. Together with the crew of their sister ship, *Helgoland,* they refused to weigh anchor. Hipper postponed sailing for twenty four hours, by which time he found that the crews of other ships had joined the mutiny. *Kronprinz Wilhelm, Friedrich der Grosse* and *Grosser Kurfürst* remained at anchor. Bitterly, Admiral von Hipper abandoned the sortie, ultimately negotiating for his own safety with the mutineers.

Markgraf was sent to Kiel with other ships of Squadron III to allow her crew to cool off and be re-institutionalised. On arrival there, 180 members of her crew were arrested and imprisoned ashore. As word spread, hostility was aroused amongst shore-based crews, resulting in further mutiny spreading to dockyard workers and civilians. A naval stoker from the Wik barracks addressed a meeting of 20,000, imploring support for the release of the 180 men from *Markgraf.* Feelings ran high and the incensed crowd marched on the prison to free the men. They were met by an armed squad of loyal sailors from a Torpedo Boat division, who fired into the crowd, killing eight and wounding twenty-one. This was the first blood of the revolution, which ultimately incited the final collapse of the Kaiser's Imperial Germany.

At the meeting of the opposing Fleets on November 21st, *Markgraf* was the penultimate ship in the German battleship line, behind *Kronprinz Wilhelm* and ahead of *Grosser Kurfürst.* Manned by a particularly strong faction of revolutionaries, the ship deteriorated into a dilapidated and rust-streaked spectacle at Scapa Flow. But her troubled and bloody career was not yet finished. As she settled on 21st June, 1919, as sea water flooded into her vital parts, over-enthusiastic British marines shot dead her Commanding Officer, Korvettenkapitän Walther Schumann, and a Chief Petty Officer, Hermann Dittmann, as they attempted to prevent the British from boarding the stricken ship.

As is demonstrated from observations of the lie of her masts and anchor cables, the once mighty *Markgraf* dipped her bows beneath the water throwing her stern in the air as she rolled over to port, sliding beneath the waves with forward momentum. Her prow furrowed into the seabed stopping her slide. Her stern finally submerged beneath the surface forever amidst waterspouts, whirlpools and great boiling gushes of air erupting to the surface.

Diving on MARKGRAF

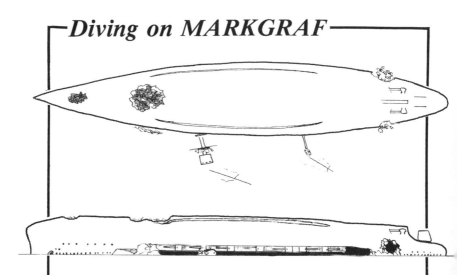

The last Battleship to sink, *Markgraf* disappeared at 16.45 and settled starboard side uppermost in position **N 58° 53' 31", W 03° 09' 55"**. Today, her superstructure is sunk deeply into the seabed as her weight continues to force her over.

The diver arrives at the end of the shotline (at a depth of 24 metres,) beside the rusty weight anchoring it down. The bottom is flat and featureless except for brown weed, anemones, and an occasional small crab. He realises that he is on the upturned hull of *Markgraf,* and fins away from the shotline, soon arriving at a bilge keel. Finning over this, the hull suddenly drops away below. Following it down, he passes over a joint in the plating — the lower edge of the hull side armour. Down further, a gun barrel is protruding from beneath the ship. The torch beam follows the barrel along to a turret, recognised as that of a 5.9-inch casemate gun. It fits snugly into the armoured casemate bulkhead with the empty squares of the gunlayer's telescope viewing ports staring blackly.

Descending to the seabed, the gun turret and the planking of the weatherdeck below the turret top, (now directly over the diver), is only sparsely covered in the sponge-like growth called Dead Men's Fingers. The caulking between the individual planks is clearly visible in torchlight, and a black void between the weatherdeck and the seabed extends so far beneath the hull that the torch beam fades into the impenetrable distance. Venturing under the ship, in blackness only penetrated by torchlight, open doors and lights in the forward superstructure reveal the remains of wireless installations, switch and fuseboxes on the bulkheads. Amazingly, a candle is floating on the deck above the diver which must have been there since 1919! The diver retreats to fin aft, clean deck planking above, until the midships 12-inch gun turret is found half-buried in the shale. Aft again is the starboard crane stanchion. Finning out from beneath the hull, the diver passes under an open hatch blocked with large lumps of coal fallen from the bunkers above.

Forward the foremast is located, the spotting top intact but stripped of instruments by the Germans before the final voyage. All that remains inside are electric plugs suspended on brass flexible conduit, and switchboxes on the bulkheads. Moving back to the hull, (the depth gauge now reading 43 metres,) the diver fins left, the hull side looming above to the right and disappearing into the haze. The space between deck and seabed narrows as he moves along the ship, until the hull side meets the seabed. Portholes, many of which are open, form a line along the hull plating. Massive slabs of hull side armour plate lean against the hull or lie flat on the seabed where fallen from their rotted mountings. Soon the hull side sweeps down in a gentle curve to the sea floor, this being the flare built to deflect heavy seas from washing over the forepart. Now the diver arrives at an anchor chain hawse — a large rimmed tunnel in the bow side, with the massively linked, studded chain still running out and along the seabed, to loop back over the hull. Standing at the prow, the diver looks up to see the curve of the bow rising above as the blunt ram shape overhangs him.

Finning up, the diver arrives at the bow torpedo tube to find the hull blown open, no doubt to recover the many non-ferrous fittings from within the torpedo room. Tangled wreckage fills this wound, which extends for about thirty feet aft. The diver locates a bilge keel to avoid becoming disorientated on the flat hull, and at this point probably finishes the dive for the day.

The following day he locates the bilge keel again, and finning to his left, follows it in a seemingly interminable swim. Finally it leads slightly down to an area of further demolition work in the region of the propeller shaft stern tubes, where twisted hull plates surround agonisingly-shaped wreckage inside. Past this and further below, is the stern bottom aft of the stern tubes. Finning right, he drops down to the seabed, finding the quarterdeck flat on the silty bottom. He fins round the curve of the stern, lined with portholes, and along the port side to where salvage work has left a huge hole in the hull side. The diver can swim right through, beneath propeller shafts high above and passing over wreckage of steering gear, pumps and pipework. He emerges on the starboard side having been joined on his sojourn by wrasse and goldsinny feeding off the stirred sediment. He now fins up the vertical hull side, and passing the twin rudders catches a last glimpse of *Markgraf* as he heads for his first decompression stop.

Chapter 5
BRUMMER

BEFORE THE GREAT WAR the major countries had been searching for weapons which could be used against potential enemy shipping without the many costs of maintaining a fleet at sea. The mine was recognised as an excellent weapon of both offence and defence. Fields laid off a country's own bases with secret channels were a deterrent to an attacking enemy fleet, and minefields laid off enemy bases could disable or sink units of the enemy's fleet. Offensive minefields achieved considerable success for both sides during the course of the war. The light cruisers *Brummer* and *Bremse* were designed to lay such minefields. The ships could work alone, sowing deadly seeds of destruction close to enemy shores, as they had the swiftness to outrun any vessel which could overpower them with gunfire. They also had enough firepower to sink the smaller but faster destroyers which were the only ships capable of catching them.

Seiner Majestät Minendampfer (His Majesty's Minesteamer) *Brummer* was designed as early as 1913 and built at the Vulcan Shipyard, Stettin, on the Baltic coast. Her propulsion machinery had been designed and built for the Russian Battlecruiser *Navarin,* but Germany was at war before completing the order, and utilised the turbines for *Brummer* and her sister *Bremse.* The Russian *Navarin* was never completed, but *Brummer* was commissioned and joined the Fleet in the autumn of 1916.

Brummer carried 360 mines, three times as many as any other German cruiser, and a formidable cargo. To compensate, however, she had only half as many guns, carrying four 5·9-inch quick firing units. They were in single turrets all mounted on the ship's centreline so that all could be used when firing broadsides. Crews manning the guns were protected only by a

▲
SMS
Brummer
21st Nov.
1918
(Imperial
War
Museum)

41

simple shield, open at the rear and exposing the gun loaders in particular. Additionally, *Brummer* carried two 3·4-inch anti-aircraft mounts between the after funnel and the mainmast, and two torpedo launchers, one each side of the upper deck and abeam of the forefunnel.

Brummer was also lightly armoured. The protective belt of armour plate along the ship's sides, which also served as hull plating was only 1·5 inches thick, and her deck plating was only ⅜ inch thick. Since British destroyers carried only 4-inch guns, it was considered unlikely that *Brummer* would ever be on the receiving end of their shells. Anyway, her main guns could outrange any such attackers, and her high speed of 34 knots would soon leave behind any ship capable of out-gunning her.

Her gracefully curved bow, an unusual feature for German light cruisers, simulated that of the British *Arethusa*-class cruisers, and she could masquerade as one by lowering her mainmast. (Other features, however, such as her tall, slim funnels, would have given her away.) The long, low, uncluttered deck spaces and elegantly raked masts and funnels made *Brummer* look the thoroughbred she was. Nevertheless, she was a utility ship, fitted out as Germany's industry began to run short of materials. Many otherwise non-ferrous fittings had to be made from iron or steel; brass and gunmetal being reserved for various engine-room components. It was also sparse below decks. With her fine hull lines, however, and foaming cream bow waves she still made an impressive sight when steaming at full speed.

Brummer's propulsion machinery comprised two turbines each directly coupled to its own propeller and arranged in tandem within the hull. The forward turbine powered the port propeller anti-clockwise, and the after turbine drove the starboard propeller clockwise. The turbines developed 46,000 horsepower. Steam was provided from six boilers, four oil-fired and two coal-fired, arranged singly fore and aft along the ship's centreline. Oil was carried for the boilers in the vessel's double bottom tanks, and coal within the longitudinal bunkers along the ship's sides, where they gave additional protection to machinery spaces. (Electric power was supplied from two steam generators and one diesel generator.) The boilers were of larger tube diameter than the capital ships, and so required less maintenance. This was in line with the concept of employing cruisers as lone raiders against Britain's commercial shipping, being supplied with fuel and ammunition from support vessels. (This practice was ultimately abandoned, as Britain's blockade of Germany prevented support vessels from breaking out to reach the cruisers.)

Displacing 4,000 tons, the ship measured 460 feet overall, and 449 feet along the waterline, (excluding bow and stern overhangs). Her maximum beam at about midships was 44 feet, and with a very fine bow entry the vessel's hull shape was designed for optimum speed. With minimal flare to the forecastle hull sides and a forward freeboard of 18 feet, she would have been a wet ship in bad weather, as her sharp bow cleaved through waves instead of rising over them.

Her 1·5-inch thick side armour plate was 7' 8" deep and 360 feet long. Together with the middle deckhead across the top of the belts, this created an internal citadel, subdivided into 15 main watertight compartments. Some of these were the width of the ship, but others were subdivided longitudinally with watertight bulkheads. Aft, an extension to the citadel, 10 feet wide and 30 feet long, enclosed the hydraulic steering gear and the 5·9-inch magazine for the aftermost gun.

The main citadel enclosed, from forward, ship's stores, anchor chain lockers, meat and food stores and the forward 5·9-inch magazine. Behind this, directly beneath the bridge, was the diesel generator room. Aft were the six boiler rooms, one behind the other, and the two steam turbine rooms. Behind were the 2 steam generator rooms beneath the after superstructure.

The hull contained three main decks. The bottom platform deck housed propulsion turbines, boilers and generator rooms and magazines. The middle deck was the main mine storage area with boiler flues and ventilators (supplying forced draught to the boiler fires) the centre. The over or upper deck also stored mines, with flue and ventilator ducting, the ship's bakery and engineers' mess rooms all in the centre. As with most ships, accommodation for ratings was forward, in *Brummer* on the upper 2 decks within the forecastle. The 457 men messed at long bench tables, slept in hammocks, and were provided with communal showers. Such accommodation was basic, but standard in most navies. The 23 officers slept aft, and many had their own cabins with bunks and desks, and messed in fine manner off china plates served by stewards. The Commanding Officer had his own bathroom complete with full size bath, while more junior officers shared bathrooms.

On each side of the upper deck, mines were carried within timber cradles and mounted on trolleys which ran on pairs of rails. The middle deck had two sets of these rails on each side of the boiler flue and ventilator trunking. The rails on the upper deck extended aft from within the deckhouses along the quarter-deck, and branched into two pairs of rails, terminating in four launching ramps. One pair was on each side of the kedge anchor on the extreme stern, and the second pair some twenty feet forward of these, which launched their mines over each side of the quarterdeck. Four elevators hoisted mines from the middle to the upper deck while they were being laid, thus ensuring a steady supply. Once launched, the mine, with its mooring rope and sinker, would sink to the seabed still housed in the timber cradle. *43*

The cradle was held together with screws inserted into salt plugs, which would dissolve and finally release the buoyant mine. A mooring rope attached to the weight on the seabed, arrested the mine's ascent at a predetermined depth. There it would lurk unseen until activated when touched by a passing ship's hull.

In October, 1917, *Brummer* and *Bremse* took part in what was then considered to be a particularly ruthless action against commercial shipping supplying Britain. Admiral Scheer had devised the plan to distract the British Admiralty from the German landings on the Baltic islands, and to strike a blow against Britain's command of the North Sea trade routes.

One of Admiral Jellicoe's first tasks as Second Lord of the Admiralty, was to institute a convoy system for merchant ships supplying Britain, with each convoy protected by escorting destroyers. Reports from German U-boats said that frequent convoys from Shetland to Norway were escorted by only two or three destroyers — sufficient to inhibit U-boats, but vulnerable to larger and better-armed surface ships. Thus, early on the 16th October, 1917, *Brummer* and *Bremse* slipped from their moorings in the Jade River, to intercept a convoy en route from Bergen to Lerwick. The merchant ships were protected by two armed trawlers, *Elise* and *P.Fannon,* and two 'M' class destroyers, HMS *Mary Rose* and HMS *Strongbow,* (armed with three 4-inch and one 2-pounder gun each). The convoy was under the command of Lieutenant Commander C. L. Fox on *Mary Rose,* which was steaming some eight miles ahead of the leading ship. *Strongbow,* under Lieutenant Commander Brooke, was behind the convoy.

As dawn broke on the 17th October, *Brummer* surprised and decimated *Strongbow* almost before her men had time to leave their hammocks. Her first salvo severed the main steam pipes from boilers to turbines and the ship stopped, to be pounded time and again by the guns of both *Brummer* and *Bremse*. Those of the crew still able to do so, abandoned *Strongbow* as she sank at 07.30. Only one 4-inch shell from her guns struck *Brummer* on her side plating at the joint with the forecastle deck.

Meanwhile, HMS *Mary Rose,* hearing gunfire from astern, turned back at full speed. Soon within sight of the German cruisers, *Mary Rose* was also outgunned and sunk. The totally outclassed trawlers, (fitted with two-pounder guns) together with three merchant ships made good their escape. (*Elise* later returned to pick up the few survivors. Those from *Mary Rose* eventually reached shore not far from Bergen in Norway.) *Brummer* under the command of Kapitän Leonhardi, and *Bremse,* commanded by Kapitän Westerkamp, then turned their guns on the merchant ships, without giving their crews a chance to abandon ship. Their work finished, a few salvoes were fired at the unfortunate survivors of *Strongbow* before they sped off south to safety.

The trawler, *P.Fannon,* and the three merchant ships arrived at Lerwick later in the day to report the massacre — none had radio equipment on board with which to alert the rest of the British Fleet. British Command therefore knew nothing of the German cruisers' presence until it was too late to try to intercept them.

The survivors of the merchant ships were left to their fate by the Germans — reinforcing world opinion that Germany's sea warfare was inhuman. They had been already condemned for U-boat attacks on unarmed merchant ships. Admiral Scheer, however, considered the attack so successful that it was repeated two months later using large torpedo boat destroyers. Germany now considered reverting to the former policy of using her cruisers as lone commerce raiders. *Brummer* and *Bremse* were to have their bunker spaces increased and break through Britain's blockade into the Atlantic to play havoc with her commercial shipping.

As Scheer had intended, Britain added heavier ships to her convoy escorts. But the plan to erode Britain's numerical advantage by attacking these ships with larger units never materialised. America at this time entered the war, boosting Britain's Fleet by six Dreadnought battleships and numerous smaller ships. This rendered the position of Germany's surface Fleet almost hopeless. The plans to use *Brummer* and *Bremse* as lone raiders was finally shelved as the chances of their being successful became so unlikely in the face of this opposition.

At the meeting of the Fleets on 21st November, 1918, *Brummer* was fifth ship in the line of German cruisers under the divisional command of Kommodör Korder. After inspection in the Firth of Forth, she arrived at Scapa Flow at the end of her last voyage on Wednesday, 27th November. Her caretaker crew must have suffered privations during the cold winter months of 1918-19 as the ship was not designed to accommodate crews for long periods.

─Diving on BRUMMER─

At 13.05 on Saturday, June 21st, 1919, *Brummer*
disappeared forever beneath the calm surface of Scapa
Flow. Listing as she sank, she finally settled on the gently
sloping seabed on her starboard side in position **N 58° 53'
50", W 03° 09' 07"**. Her stern lies in 34-37 metres and her
bow in 31-34 metres dependent upon the tide.

Light intensity fades as the diver heads down the
shotline into the forbidding gloom, becoming brighter as he
suddenly lands on the pale grey flatness of the hull. A row
of scuttles to the left stretch into the hazy distance,
covered, as is the hull side, with myriads of tiny fronds of
brown seaweed, diminutive bright anemones and spindly
Brittle Starfish. Finning along the row of portholes he
suddenly arrives at the bow, and from the prow on his
right, the stony seabed is just discernible below. The
graceful arch of *Brummer's* bow sweeps away to the left,
with its sharp bow entry and slight ram shape at the
forefoot. From the seabed, the whole shape is silhouetted
above against the bright green light penetrating from the
surface. Beneath the starboard side of the hull, a detached
plate is hanging. Swimming under the overhanging bow to
go through the hole, the diver reaches the upper deck
within the forecastle, once mess rooms and accommodation
for the crew. Forward are the anchor chain hawse pipes,
the noise from which must have deafened those in the
forecastle as the chains rattled through. Deck support
columns are placed conveniently around for the diver to
lean on as he takes stock of his situation.

A hatch leads through to the middle deck, and easily
slipping through, the diver is almost in darkness. Torchlight

picks out more deck support columns and faint light just reaches through the portholes in the ship's side above him. Spindles for operating valves in the ship's bottom pass through this deck, their connections so corroded, (or perhaps deliberately loosened to prevent the ship being saved), that an accidental knock sends them crashing down below and sending up clouds of disturbed silt.

Another hatch leads to the platform deck, but it is too small to enter. Torchlight, however, picks out the remains of rotted tarpaulins and ropes, this having been one of the stores. Aft on the left, mounds of anchor chain spill out through the now disintegrated chain locker bulkheads. No portholes cast their eery light into this compartment, (below the waterline when the ship floated,) and the thickening clouds of disturbed silt persuade the diver to leave.

Passing back through the middle deck hatch, a hole is spotted in the forecastle deck which leads outside the hull. Here, the anchor chains hang across the vertical teak deck, with the solid mahogany strips behind where the chains used to lie. Finning aft, with the deck to the diver's right, he passes the anchor chain capstans and the muzzle of the forward 5·9-inch gun aiming directly at him. Passing along the barrel and over the protective shield, he reaches the conning tower — the command centre when the ship was in battle. This armoured structure has horizontal viewing slits and is crowned with the arms of the gun central control rangefinder. (Magnifying lenses and reflective prisms were removed from this before the ship left Germany.)

The access door down behind the conning tower is open, but the space inside empty save for silt which soon reduces visibility to zero. Facing the door, to the left, is the bridge. Empty square windows stare, and the signal deck handrails above the bridge windows support fallen rigging wires. The rear of the bridge has been removed for salvage divers to gain access. Aft of the bridge, a large hole in the upper deck reveals armoured gratings, fitted at the base of the forefunnel space to prevent plunging shells from entering the foremost boiler flues. The bent and buckled plating that was the funnel lies below on the seabed.

Aft again stands the mid-mounted 5·9-inch gun, barrel pointing dead astern. The empty breech lies behind the protective shield, the closing block removed while *Brummer* was prepared for her rendezvous with the British Fleet. Further aft lies the smashed remains of the ship's boiler and engine rooms. Blasted by salvage divers, platform gratings, pump castings, electric motors, junction boxes and twisted, severed piping, spill from the dis-embowelled hull across the seabed.

Past this mayhem is the still intact stern superstructure. The A-shaped pedestals of the emergency steering position remain, and aft, loosened hull plating has fallen across the superimposed after 5·9-inch gun. Only the breech and muzzle protrude from beneath this plating, unless the diver moves underneath. Further aft again, the aftermost 5·9-inch gun on the quarterdeck points directly astern. The hull is broken open in this area, the quarterdeck planking blasted out. Inside lie the remains of cabinets, tables and various fittings from the officers' accommodation, smashed and heaped in confusion and more than half-buried in the thick silt on the bottom.

Finning from beneath the fragile hull plates to the stern, the kedge anchor is still in place in its hawse. Round the curve of the stern, the rudder lies flat on the seabed. Above on the hull side is the empty port propeller shaft bearing pedestal, no propeller or shaft remaining. (The bronze of the propeller, and the ease of access probably made these items some of the first to be salvaged.)

Thus the diver leaves *Brummer* to return to the real world above. His memories, however, will be all the richer for this short visit to these historical and impressive remains.

BRUMMER

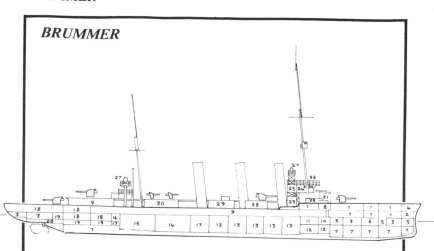

1	Crew spaces	11	Diesel generator	21	Conning tower
2	Hammock lockers	12	Magazines	22	Ready use
3	Stores	13	Boiler room		ammunition
4	Cells and	14	Port shaft turbine	23	Watch officers
	hammock lockers	15	Starboard shaft		cabin
5	Cable lockers		turbine	24	Compass platform
6	Capstan machinery	16	Turbo-generator	25	Chart house
7	Fuel oil		room	26	Signal bridge
8	Galley	17	Steering engine	27	Searchlight
9	Mine stowage	18	Officers accom.		platform
10	Lower control	19	Magazines	28	Bakery and galley
	room	20	Rudder machinery	29	Radio room
				30	Workshops

Chapter 6
KARLSRUHE

A SECOND class cruiser of the *Königsberg II*-class, Seiner Majestät Kleine Kreuzer (His Majesty's Small Cruiser) *Karlsruhe,* joined the High Seas Fleet on November 15th, 1916, having been fitting out for almost 12 months. The vessel was launched without any ceremony on the 31st January 1916, from a slipway at the Imperial Dockyard at Wilhelmshaven, (builders of the Battleship *König* three years before). She was built as Ersatz (replacement for) *Niobe,* an ageing light cruiser of 1899. The addition of five such cruisers to the Fleet during 1916 was most welcome to German High Command, as 17 second and third class cruisers had been lost between commencement of hostilities and June 1st, 1916.

Allocated to the Second Scouting Group of the Fleet following her commissioning and 'shaking-down' period, *Karlsruhe's* commander was Fregattenkapitän Tietgens, who was to remain with her until the voyage to internment.

Karlsruhe and the three other ships of her class; *Emden II, Königsberg II* and *Nürnberg II,* were a vast improvement on their predecessors. They were faster and carried guns of larger calibre and greater range. They were also fitted with the compact turbine engines to afford greater space for fuel and ammunition, and to increase their operating range and fighting power.

Karlsruhe was only the third big German warship to be fitted with geared turbines. The year before, some torpedo boat destroyers and the light cruisers, *Frankfurt* and *Wiesbaden,* had been so equipped to great advantage. Subsequently, they were adopted for all light cruisers. These sophisticated engines produced a massive 45,000 horsepower to drive *Karlsruhe* through two propellers to 28.5 knots — sometimes more when

▲
SMS
Karlsruhe
(Author's
collection)

50

the boilers were forced beyond their normal working pressure. Steam was supplied from ten coal-fired water tube boilers, and two oil-fired boilers (only used when optimum speed was required). Coal was supplied from bunkers arranged longitudinally along the ship's sides, and oil was carried in double bottom tanks.

Approximately equivalent to the British Town-class cruisers, (but longer, more powerful and faster), *Karlsruhe* and her sisters could carry 120 mines in addition to their more conventional armament. These mines were carried in the open on the after deck and launched from ramps on each side of the stern just forward of the anchor.

Accommodation for most of the officers was on the after end of the middle deck. On the upper deck, more accommodation, ward rooms and saloons were within the after deckhouse, and the Commander's large cabin was at the after end on the starboard side. (All had large, square windows covered with steel shutters as defence against shell splinters). Senior officers each had their own cabins, but from the rank of Lieutenant down, officers shared two to a cabin.

Accommodation for ratings was forward, within the forecastle on the upper two decks. The men slept in hammocks and messed at long tables, (about 12 men at each), and their meals were cooked in a large galley aft of the foremast on the upper deck. The officers' galley, providing different rations, was in the afterpart of the centre deckhouse. This deckhouse also accommodated the senior engineers' cabins, washing and laundry rooms and the paymaster's quarters. Considerable space was also taken up by ventilator ducting and boiler exhaust trunking, as the after boiler rooms were below this area. The forward deckhouse contained laundry and drying rooms, the ship's bakery and the engineers' workshops. The bulk of it, however, was taken up by forced draught and boiler flue ducting for the boiler rooms two decks below.

Karlsruhe carried eight 5.9-inch guns each in single mountings. On the forecastle deck, two were housed to port and starboard, and one on either side of the ship just forward of the latticework bridge wing supporting structure. There was one to port and starboard further aft on the quarterdeck, (abeam of the after end of the centre deckhouse); one on the superstructure deck of the after deckhouse, and one on the quarterdeck. Two 3.4-inch high elevation guns in single mounts were housed on the superstructure deck of the centre deckhouse, between the after funnel and the main mast. In addition, two 50cm torpedo tubes were fitted on the upper deck, one each side of the ship abeam of the forefunnel. Two further torpedo tubes were fitted underwater on the platform deck forward of machinery spaces.

Four powerful carbon arc searchlights were mounted   *51*

individually on platforms on the fore and main masts. Those on the foremast were remotely controlled from the signal bridge deck, and those on the mainmast were similarly controlled through mechanical linkages from a platform at the base of the mast. An emergency steering position was provided between the mainmast and the 5.9-inch gun on the superstructure deck of the after deckhouse. The main control position was, of course, within the bridge. A battle station, however, with all navigation, steering, engine and boiler room telegraphs, was housed within the armoured conning tower, and repeated below the armoured deck. The gun rangefinder was on top of the conning tower, but each gun was provided with telescopic optical sights so that they could be individually operated if necessary.

The *Königsberg II's* were larger vessels than previous German light cruisers. They were nearly 497 feet long overall, with a beam of 47 feet and displacing 7,125 tons when fully loaded. They required a crew of 475 men and 25 officers. Pleasing to the eye, as were most later German ships, they had a fine rake to their bow, and considerable flare to the hull sides aft of the bow. Midships, the deck spaces were uncluttered save for large ventilators, and seven boats served with large curved davits of heavy riveted construction.

The funnel bases were spread to accommodate the boiler flue trunking which was angled up from below, and the funnels were armour plated to about a third of their height. This was to protect against enemy shells severing the flues low down with resultant loss of gas extraction draught and boiler efficiency. The bows supported a Hall type bower anchor on each side, with a kedge anchor of similar pattern housed in a recess on the port side foredeck. A stern anchor was provided with its own hawse. Distinctive cast fairleads were fitted on the very point of the bow to accommodate mooring ropes when the ship was berthed, and could be used as guides for towing ropes if necessary. Anchor chain capstans adorned the bow to port and starboard, with a single one aft on the quarterdeck. Each was driven by its own electric motor through open gears mounted within the ship, two decks below.

Scouting Division II was commanded by Kontre (Rear) Admiral von Reuter — (later famous as the man who sank the greatest tonnage of shipping ever in a single day). As a unit of Scouting Division II, *Karlsruhe* was assigned to cover for minesweepers operating in the German Bight. Frequent operations were undertaken by these ships to maintain safe passage for the German ships through minefields being continuously laid by the British. The cruisers of Scouting Division II would be detached to defend the lightly armed and slow minesweepers against attacks from British light forces.

On the 16th August, 1917, the light cruisers *Karlsruhe* and

Frankfurt were detached together with a number of torpedo boat destroyers to cover minesweeping operations in the German Bight. A flotilla of British destroyers surprised the minesweeping group, but before any damage was inflicted to either side, they left, being outnumbered and outgunned by the German ships. Early in September, *Karlsruhe* and the Second Scouting Group retired to the Baltic to carry out exercises together, (and to keep the ships away from the disruptive elements plagueing the Fleet).

Immediately after these manouevres, the force joined the fleet for the action against the Baltic Islands. In a massive push into Russian occupied territory, the German 8th Army had advanced as far as the Gulf of Riga, a large bay in the Baltic east coast. Its narrow entrance was guarded by a group of islands — principally Oesel, the largest and southernmost, Dagoe to the north-west and Moon to the north-east, (connected to Oesel by a short causeway). Russian infantry divisions had guns from 6 to 12-inch calibre trained on all the narrows into the Gulf of Riga, and heavy units of the Russian Baltic Fleet sheltered in bays on the east of the Islands. In order to attack these ships, the Germans had to occupy the Islands themselves. Thus, a seaborne invasion was planned to start from Libau (on the coast of Courland), and some divisions of the 8th Army were sent there along with some naval units. These included the battleships of Squadron II and IV, the battlecruiser *Moltke,* (as Flagship of the operation's Naval Commander, Rear Admiral Erhardt Schmidt), the light cruisers of the Second Scouting Group under Rear Admiral von Reuter, and a large number of torpedo boat destroyers and minesweepers. In addition, 19 merchant steamers were to transport the 25,000 officers and men, 8,500 horses, 2,500 vehicles, 40 field guns, 200 machine guns and 80 mortars, together with the 2,300 tons of supplies necessary to keep the troops victualled.

Scouting Group II joined the massed ships at Libau on 25th September. The first task assigned to *Karlsruhe* was to transport men of Vortrupp I to Putziger Inlet, (from where they would go to the invasion on *Moltke,* whose base was there). She then returned to Libau for exercises in embarking and landing troops, horses and equipment. On the 10th October, she embarked two officers and 78 men of the Fourth Sachsen Cyclist Battalion, (together with their bicycles), and anchored off Libau overnight. She was appointed Flagship of the Second Transport Group, comprising five merchant ships and a strong force of protective torpedo boat destroyers. The minesweeping flotillas were to advance first, followed by *Moltke* and the Third Squadron of Battleships, screened by numerous torpedo boats.

The massed Fleet set sail on the 11th October, the big ships following the diminutive minesweepers. The Russians had used minelaying to good effect; dense fields had been laid in the various straights and bays suitable for enemy landings, including Tagga Bay. Due to the slow progress of the minesweepers, however, Rear Admiral Schmidt ordered the Fleet to pass them, afraid of losing the element of surprise. By amazing good fortune, his entire Fleet passed through the minefield at the entrance to Tagga Bay via a narrow gap not known to the Germans. (The Battleships *Bayern* and *Grosser Kurfürst,* however, struck mines as they prepared to shell the gun fortifications overlooking the landing place. Although damaged, they completed their part in the expedition.)

While the big ships set about destroying the shore batteries, *Karlsruhe* led her transport fleet through the Bay of Tagga and disembarked her passengers on their bicycles. The German troops came under fire from Russian field guns hidden in woodland further inshore, but these were finally silenced by the 5.9-inch and 4.1-inch guns of the light cruisers and torpedo boat destroyers. (Their fall of shot was reported back to the ships by an observation aircraft — the first time the Germans has adopted this method of spotting).

During the remainder of the invasion, *Karlsruhe* acted as scout and protection for the Battleships of Squadron IV, (the *Kaiser*-class ships), which were deployed in destroying more Russian land batteries about the islands' coasts. By October 17th, the Germans had control of Oesel and many Russian troops were taken prisoner. (The ships of the German Squadron IV, with *Karlsruhe* in attendance, were detailed to force the heavily-mined Moon Sound to cut off the escape route to the mainland, but bad weather forced them to abandon the plan.) The Navy's work finished, *Karlsruhe* escorted 10 of the merchant ships of the transport squadron back to Libau, from where she returned to Wilhelmshaven to resume her North Sea duties. Inactive for the following weeks, she was taken into dry dock on 11th November for hull cleaning and minor repairs.

Karlsruhe's next sortie was at the beginning of April, 1918, when she was detailed to cover the light cruisers *Bremse* and *Arcona* as they laid offensive minefields in advance of the planned interception of Allied convoys off Norway. As recounted elsewhere, following the loss of a propeller on the battlecruiser *Moltke,* the sortie was abandoned and the ships returned to their bases.

The following month, *Karlsruhe* was minelaying at the eastern edge of the Hoofden. She later served as escort cruiser to the Fleet Flagship, *Baden,* during a visit by the Grand Duke Friedrich II of Baden. Following more exercises in the Baltic, *Karlsruhe* returned to Wilhelmshaven and thence to dry dock once again. During the German evacuation of their U-boat and destroyer bases established at Zeebrugge and Bruges in October, 1918, *Karlsruhe* stood off the coast of Flanders as guard against attack by British ships. This did not materialise, as by this time the Allies' main Naval pre-occupation was the U-boat problem.

For her final voyage, *Karlsruhe* was Flagship of the Second Scouting Group under the command of Kapitän zur See Harder. She was lead ship of the line of cruisers, ahead of *Frankfurt* and two miles astern of *Grosser Kurfürst,* the last in the line of Dreadnoughts. As the Fleets met, the British *Arethusa*-class crusier, HMS *Phaeton,* took station ahead of *Karlsruhe* to lead her into the Firth of Forth. She was flanked to port by the battleships of the British Fourth Battle Squadron, and to starboard by the American battleships of the Sixth Squadron. She sailed the following week escorted by battleships of the British First Battle Squadron, and anchored to the north-west of the island of Cava.

Diving on KARLSRUHE

Karlsruhe's reduced crew endured the winds and driving rain of the winter of 1918-19 before sending her to the bottom in position **N 58° 53' 23", W 03° 11' 18"**. She now lies on her starboard side in 24-27 metres, depending on the tide. A little tide flows from Hoy Sound and over Bring Deeps into Scapa Flow, ensuring better underwater visibility on this wreck than on any of the remaining German ships.

After his descent, the diver swims ahead along the flat plates to a bulwark beneath which a pair of mooring bollards protrude from the vertical deck. Below them is a rise in the deck, and deeper still is the tall, round structure of the conning tower, (from where the ship and gunlaying were controlled when in action). Over the edge of the hull is a drop across the steel deck which leads to the side of the

conning tower. The bridge structure is on the right.
Between the conning tower and the bridge, the access door
to the tower is closed, but hangs vertically, loose on its
hinges. Made of 4-inch thick armour plate, the door is too
heavy to open, but there is a small opening at the top of
the conning tower through which torchlight picks out the
shapes of a compass binnacle and telegraphs beneath
encrustations of marine growth.

Leaving the conning tower, the diver fins forward along
the seabed, passing over wire hawsers and steel plate,
broken and fallen from a small deckhouse. The starboard
forward 5.9-inch gun is found lying broken from its
mounting on the seabed, but the port gun is still in position
above. Finning up the vertical deck, torchlight inside the
protective shield of the gun reveals the end of the recoil
cylinder above the barrel. Round the shield to the barrel,
the muzzle is blanked off with a wooden plug, known as a
tompion. The corroded remains of the escutcheon, which
would have borne the coat of arms of the ship, are in
place. Dropping down to the seabed again and finning
forward towards the bow, the anchor chain capstans are
ahead and above. The anchor chains lie across the foredeck
finally disappearing into their hawse pipes. Past these is the
prow, dominated by the cast fairleads for mooring or
towing hawsers, and covered with growths of Dead Men's
Fingers and anemones. The bow is almost flat on the
seabed, (the hull obviously broken further aft). Finning
along the shape, some hull side plating has been removed,
exposing the hull frames and longitudinal stringers which
form the skeleton of the ship.

Aft along the ship's bottom from the foot of the bow
is an area where salvage work has torn open the bottom
plates to afford access into the platform deck. The diver
warily works his way past the twisted hull bottom frames
and bent platform deck plating, surrounded by distorted
piping, hanging electric cables and bulkheads wasted paper-
thin by corrosion. He finally finds himself in an electrical
control room of some description.

There are large brass fuse and switchboxes all around
and convolutions of heavy electric cables disappear through
still intact bulkheads. It is difficult to manoeuvre back out
in the confined and now murky space. Small spiny crabs
and flakes of rust fall down, dislodged from the plating
above by trapped exhaled air. Back on the seabed outside
the wreck, in the welcome light from above, the diver fins
up and over the hull to the port bulwark. Down over this

are the remains of the bridge. The upper bridge, which once housed the torpedo aiming rangefinders and signal lamps, has disintegrated into twisted wreckage on the seabed. Bent handrails show where the signal bridge once was, and forward, the command bridge is now empty of navigating equipment. The bridge wings still stand supported on their flimsy-looking lattice steelwork supports, but little else remains of the light and open structure.

Aft of the bridge, salvage work has demolished the hull from the upper deck through to the keel, where distorted sections of hull plating intertwine with boiler room piping, pump castings and turbine blades. A great amount of recognisable items lie within this debris, such as the odd brass fusebox, boat davits and a torpedo launcher. Brass bulkhead lamps and fuel oil bunkering pipe caps litter the area beneath electric cables, boiler fire gratings and electric motors.

Further aft, the hull becomes recognisable again. The stern is intact, and beneath the quarterdeck the accommodation area can be entered. It is empty, but dimly lit through portholes in the hull side above. Passing through rotted bulkheads and over deck support columns, the diver can fin through inside to the extreme stern. Retracing his movements, he emerges to fin aft outside the wrecked after-end. Here, the stern anchor lies partly out of its hawse and on the seabed. Round the stern is the rudder, flat on the seabed. At the top, where some hull plates are missing, are the hydraulic rams coupled to the quadrant arm on the rudder post.

This then is *Karlsruhe,* her short but relatively active life prematurely ended in 1919. Although salvage work has extensively damaged sections of the hull, her wreck is still impressive and well worth a detailed visit.

KARLSRUHE

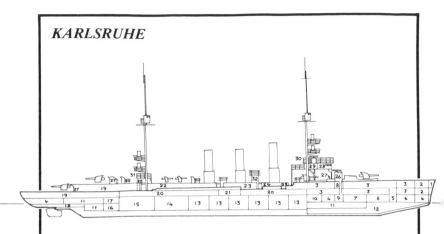

1 Cells and hammock lockers	15 Starboard shaft turbine	25 Radio room
2 Hammock locker	16 Steering engine	26 Conning tower
3 Crews' spaces	17 Turbo-generator	27 Ready use ammunition lockers
4 Stores	18 Rudder machinery	28 Compass platform
5 Cable locker	19 Officers' accom.	29 Chart house and watch officer's cabin
6 Capstan machinery	20 Coal bunkers	30 Upper bridge and torpedo director
7 Torpedo room	21 Torpedo stowage	31 Secondary gun director platform
8 Galley	22 Junior officers and engineer officers	32 Boiler room and turbine room induction vents
9 Lower control room	23 Workshops, washrooms and drying rooms	
10 Diesel generator	24 Washrooms, bakery and galley	
11 Magazines		
12 Fuel oil		
13 Boiler room		
14 Port shaft turbine		

Chapter 7
KÖLN

KÖLN II WAS LAID DOWN at the Blohm and Voss shipyard
in Hamburg off the River Elbe, and launched on the 5th
October, 1916. She was the first of the new *Dresden II*-class
cruisers to be completed and was built as a replacement for the
earlier *Köln* which was sunk at the Battle of Heligoland Bight on
the 28th August, 1914. Only one other ship of the *Dresden II*
class was completed before the war ended. Another five:
Frauenlob III, Leipzig II, Magdeburg II, Rostock II and
Wiesbaden II were not finished in time due to shortages of
materials and manpower, and priorities being given to U-boat
construction. (All Germany's cruisers were named after German
towns, their battlecruisers after German Generals and their
battleships after members of the nobility or Royalty).

As a further development from the *Königsberg II*-class
ships, the *Dresdens* were slightly larger and more complete
fighting ships. *Köln II* (hereafter referred to as *Köln*) was fitted
with eight 5.9-inch guns, each singly mounted with a protective
shield for the crews. Two were mounted side by side on the
foredeck, and could swivel through 180 degrees in each direction
to fire at an angle over the opposite side of the ship. One was
fitted at each side of the bridge structure and at foredeck level.
These swivelled through 180 degrees outboard of the ship, from
directly ahead to directly astern to fire at any angle from the side
of the ship. Another pair were abeam and to each side of the
mainmast. These were trained aft and swivelled to fire from
directly astern, to any angle outboard up to 17 degrees from
directly forward. One was mounted on the superstructure deck
aft and could fire from directly astern, to 38 degrees outboard
from the ship's centreline forward and to port or starboard.

▲

SMS
Köln
at speed
(Author's
collection)

59

These 5.9-inch guns fired a shell weighing 46 kg, so a broadside from *Köln* delivered 276kg of high explosive from the six guns capable of being brought to bear. In addition, she carried two 3.4-inch high elevation guns in single mountings, each with a simple protective shield between the mainmast and the after funnel. These guns rotated through a full 360 degrees. They elevated to fire at an angle of 80 degrees, or depressed to 10 degrees below horizontal to engage surface craft close to the ship. They fired shells weighing 9.5kg at a rate of about 10 shells per minute. All the guns were supplied with ammunition through electrically-driven hoists from the magazines to a handling area close by the gun platforms. When at sea, a small supply of shells and cordite charges were kept in lockers on deck near each gun.

Köln was the first German light cruiser to have the conning tower built within the bridge structure. This was situated aft of, and higher than, the command bridge. (Previous designs had placed the conning tower forward of, and lower than, the command bridge.) With the *Dresden*-class light cruisers, Germany followed British design and placed the rangefinder for the guns atop the conning tower higher to afford more distant viewing. This also helped to keep the external lenses clear of spray and cordite smoke. German gun spotters operating the rangefinders were supplied with a personal eyepiece, with lenses ground to suit his eyesight. If transferred to another ship he took them with him! The British spotter had just the standard lens.

The Battle of Heligoland Bight was the first major engagement of the Great War, during which the original *Köln* was lost. On 28th August, 1914, she rushed out from her base to support the German light cruisers and destroyers, beleaguered under British fire. The British were trying to draw the German big ships out and onto the guns and torpedoes of battlecruisers and submarines waiting further out to sea. In the first bout of furious fighting, things seemed to be going badly for the British until five mighty battlecruisers pounced out of the mist. *Köln* was sunk after being repeatedly hit by salvoes from *Lion,* Beatty's Flagship. Flushed with success, the British ships made for home, having sunk four German ships without losing any of their own.

With this class of cruiser, the Germans finally abandoned the expensive underwater torpedo tubes, and all four launching tubes were fitted at upper deck level. There were two each side to port and starboard of the foremast abeam the forefunnel and the other pair just aft of the aftermost funnel. Mounting these on deck meant that the tubes could be aimed over a wider angle than underwater tubes; 140 degrees against 90 degrees. The disadvantage was that the launching tubes were more vulnerable to damage from enemy gunfire. The rangefinder for the torpedo launchers was sited on a platform built around the base of the mainmast, from where the after searchlights, mounted higher up the mast, were also controlled.

Köln was designed to carry a similar number of mines as *Karlsruhe,* and accommodation for her officers was much the same, if a little roomier. As on all warships of this period, careful design of fan sizes, ventilator ducting area and boiler flue area, assured that the boiler rooms could be pressurised to provide forced draught to the boilers and increase fire temperature and gas circulation. The boilers had smaller diameter tubes than the British ones, which provided a larger surface area of water to be heated. This improved the efficiency of the heat transfer, and thus the efficiency of the boiler output compared to fuel input. The smaller tubes could also withstand higher steam pressures within them and hence greater overloading. (In action, the Germans were notorious for exceeding the designed limits of boiler pressures to achieve higher speeds). Another advantage of small bore tubes was a weight saving per square foot of heating area of some nine or ten pounds, about 30 tons per boiler. The weight saving helped the *Dresden*-class ships achieve high speeds, (and allowed more protective armour plate on the capital ships). *Köln* recorded over 29 knots on her trials, but could have exceeded this by a considerable margin if necessary. The disadvantage of small tube boilers was that they required more attention. The tubes were susceptible to build-up of scale and blocked more frequently than the large tubes, which meant the ship was out of service for re-tubing more often. This was less acceptable to Britain, who had to be always ready to face an enemy fleet which chose to foray out from its bases.

The steam supplied from *Köln's* boilers was fed to two triple stage turbines which drove their own propeller shafts through precision gears to step down the speed of rotation. Initially, turbines were directly coupled to their propeller shafts, so that everything rotated at the same speed. Later, a gearbox was introduced between the turbine rotor shaft and the propeller shaft, ensuring that turbine blade design could be modified to utilise the high velocity of the steam. With the resultant increase in efficiency, the propellers themselves could be re-designed so that the blade angle was more conducive to driving the ship. *Köln's* propeller efficiency was increase from 42% to 50% using geared turbines, and fuel savings of up to 25% were made. This outweighed the initial extra outlay, and such systems became standard for ships of both navies later in the war.

Köln joined the Fleet during January, 1918, as a unit of the   *61*

Second Scouting Group. She patrolled in Heligoland Bight, escorting U-boats along the swept channels through Germany's defensive minefields and laying occasional strings of mines herself. At the beginning of October, 1918, her commander, Freggatenkapitän Erich Raeder, was promoted and replaced by Freggatenkapitän Kaulhausen, and she spent the first weeks of October in dry dock undergoing routine maintenance.

Following Admiral von Hipper's failed attempt at the end of October, 1918, to take the Fleet out to provoke a final battle with the British, the German ships were dispersed in an attempt to isolate the revolutionary crews. By Wednesday, 6th November, the revolution on land which had begun at Kiel, had spread across Germany to Wilhelmshaven. Led by Stoker Kuhnt, the shore-based sailors joined the dockyard workers and, unopposed, freed the sailors imprisoned after the earlier mutiny. Those on the light cruisers of Scouting Group II, however, remained loyal and put to sea to escape the revolutionary movement. The following morning a patrolling seaplane reported to Commodore Harder in *Königsberg* (which was in company with *Köln, Graudenz* and four torpedo boat destroyers), that two British cruisers with five destroyers had been spotted off the entrance to the River Ems. Harder reported this to the battleships of Squadron I, moored at nearby Borkum, whose officers attempted to put to sea in support. The battleships raised steam, but the crews then mutinied, and sailed instead to Wilhelhelmshaven. *Köln* and her consorts failed to find the British ships. With no orders to follow, she remained offshore, futilely patrolling outside the German minefields while waiting for events to take their course ashore.

Köln was finally ordered to join the internment Fleet, and berthed at Wilhelmshaven where many of her crew left the ship, including her commander. He was replaced by Kapitän-Leutnant Heinemann who remained with the ship to her end. She was unloaded of ammunition in preparation for her final voyage. Neglected and overworked during the events of past weeks, her condenser tubes were leaking at the outset of the voyage to internment, and *Köln's* resultant slow speed held up the progress of the Fleet. She was finally left some miles out of position, but eventually arrived at the Firth of Forth under escort of the British light cruiser, HMS *Chester*. *Köln's* end came at 13.50 on that eventful Saturday in July 1919, when she made a final plunge, stern first and rolling to starboard as she settled. Seawater flooded into boilers, generators and control equipment destroying thousands of hours of work and care. Her skeleton crew cast off in an open cutter, joining company with the crew of *Brummer* in a similar boat until small arms fire from a drifter persuaded them to part. Bullets sprayed into the water around their boat, and realising that the British were attempting to make

them return to their ship, Captain Heinemann ordered his men
to take off their caps, whose ribbons betrayed their ship's name.

A British destroyer only narrowly escaped being struck by
Köln as she capsized, having been alongside in an attempt to
save her. Following her sinking, the crew were taken in tow by a
drifter to be placed under arrest on board HMS *Revenge,*
Flagship of the British Admiral Fremantle.

┌─*Diving on KÖLN*─────────

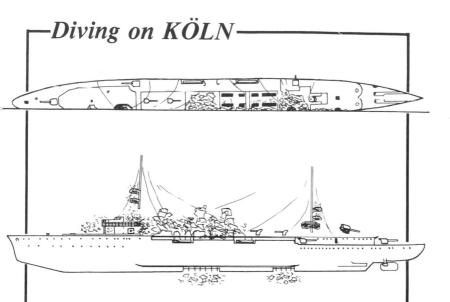

Köln settled in position **N 58° 53′ 32″, W 03° 08′ 27″.** The
divers fin down the curving plates of the hull side to the
seabed with the ship's bottom on the right. The depth
gauge reads 34 metres. They fin to an area where some hull
plates are missing, (lying on the sea floor some way from
the hull). Peering inside, the plates of the inner hull form a
barrier ahead. Pipe ends, which carried oil or fresh water,
protrude in places. Torchlight picks out heavy hull frames
to fore and aft; one is solid, forming the end of the double
bottom compartment, the other has large holes to help keep
down the weight of the ship. Backing out, they continue
along the seabed with the hull above and to the right. The
ship's bottom is again intact and there are one or two
gratings which perhaps covered seawater intakes for
condensers or fire fighting pumps. They finally arrive at the
foot of the bow, some distance clear of the seabed. Finning
beneath the hull they emerge from shadow with the flat
foredeck towering vertically above. Cables and wire ropes

litter the seabed, interspersed with some handy sized scallops! Finning aft, the starboard hull side sweeps down to the seabed, and the bulwark disappears, sinking into the shale bottom.

Continuing aft, a large hole is found in the foredeck. One diver clips his reel line to a convenient post, and edges in, and his colleague follows. Moving gently to avoid disturbing too much sediment, the divers rise inside the forecastle deck to sit astride a support column and shine their torches around. Light enters the deck from portholes in the hull side high above, but not enough to illuminate anything. (This is where the ratings slung their hammocks from the rails on the deckhead, and messed at the tables now rotted from their mountings and lying in the rubble below.) Paying out the reel line, the divers move forward and the torch beams pick out cables, pipes and bulkhead lamps. Electric switches and steel brackets still support the remains of corroded cupboards.

A hatch affords access to the next deck, and the dive leader edges through, (checking that the heavy hatch cover is not going to close behind him!) Paying out the reel line, he passes through into the upper deck. There are similar sights here and more accommodation space for the crew. Moving forward, there is a solid bulkhead, through which there is no access. The dive leader then moves back to the forecastle deck. The ladder which once gave access to the hatch in the forecastle deck is hanging below, rotted off most of its mountings. Finning forward inside the forecastle deck, there is a wasted bulkhead, where only the closely-spaced support frames remain, preventing further access. The divers then arrive back at the hole in the foredeck, to emerge once more into light.

Unclipping the reel, they fin aft again on the seabed to the conning tower. Unable to enter through the door, (due to the angle at which the ship lies,) they move round to the top where holes left by the removal of the sighting periscopes allow them to look inside. All that can be seen in the torchlight are pendulous growths of rust hanging like stalactites, which obliterate anything that may be left there. Moving forward, past the open command bridge structure and beneath, (with the steelwork of the supporting latticed column above the divers), is the remains of the watchkeeping officer's cabin. Here, reaching around steelwork and groping in corners he could not see, the author once pulled out a soft, black object which disintegrated in his hands — a book! Preserved until then in the silt, who knows what information it may have contained?

Finning aft again, (watching out for awning frames, boat davits and steel rigging wires with sharp splinters,) the 3.4-inch high elevation guns are mounted before the mainmast. The barrels are horizontal and point forward, and beneath the marine growth they appear to be almost intact. Moving aft again past the mainmast searchlight control platform and the emergency steering position, there is an open door in the topside of the aftermost deckhouse. Dropping through into the area which was officers' accommodation, and finning aft, the barbette of the after superimposed 5.9-inch gun is located. Below is a black void impenetrable by torchlight. Finning further aft, now with masses of fallen debris below, the divers reach the aftermost bulkhead of the deckhouse. The frames are too closely-spaced to allow exit, but the breech of the aftermost gun can be seen through them. Retracing their path, they emerge from the door above, and fin aft along the deckhouse side to the quarterdeck. Passing the aftermost gun they fin round the deck edge, (past the stern anchor which is still neatly in place in its hawse,) and round the stern to the rudder, flat on the seabed. Moving to the port propeller shaft bracket, they commence their ascent, left with impressive memories of the wreck.

DRESDEN II CLASS
(This layout applies to DRESDEN and KÖLN)

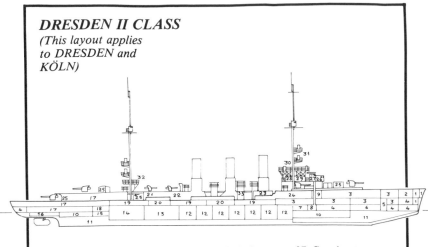

1 Hammock locker	14 Starboard shaft turbine
2 Cells and hammock lockers	15 Steering engine
3 Crews' spaces	16 Rudder machinery
4 Stores	17 Officers accom.
5 Cable locker	17 Turbo-generators
6 Capstan machinery	19 Coal bunker
7 Diesel generator	20 Torpedo stowage
8 Lower control room	21 Engineer officers
9 Galley	22 Workshops
10 Magazines	23 Galley and bakery
11 Fuel oil	24 Washing and drying room
12 Boiler room	25 Ready use ammunition
13 Port shaft turbine	26 Compass platform

27 Conning tower
28 Radio room
29 Watch officer's cabin
30 Signal bridge and torpedo director
31 Searchlight platforms
32 Secondary gunnery control platform
33 Boiler and engine room induction vents

Chapter 8
DRESDEN

THE NAMESHIP of the last class of German light cruisers to be laid down during the Great War, *Dresden II*, was built at the Howaldtswerke Dockyard at Kiel. Built as Ersatz (replacement for) *Dresden*, and launched on the 25th April, 1917, *Dresden II* was a considerably different ship from her predecessor. She was longer by over 100 feet at 510 feet overall, with a beam of 47 feet, and she displaced 7,486 tons when fully loaded. She was 'home' for 550 officers and men when at sea and was the ultimate in German light cruiser design during the Great War, being a further advance from the *Königsberg II* cruisers. The ship was powered by twin geared turbines driving two propellers with a total shaft horse power of 49,000, and she achieved 27·8 knots on trials. She was finally handed over to the Navy on the 28th March, 1918. At this time, the German Naval priority was their U-boat service and recruiting and training were principally aimed at providing crews for new U-boats (which were being commissioned at a rate of about ten per month during the first months of 1918).

The original *Dresden* was part of Vice Admiral Graf von Spee's squadron who routed the British at the Battle of Coronel, on November 1st, 1914. This was the Royal Navy's first defeat for over a century. Incensed at the defeat, the British Admiralty sent out two battlecruisers to track them down. *Dresden* was the only ship to escape from their guns when the two sides met off the Falkland Islands. She fled to Juan Fernandez Island off Chile, where she was found by British cruisers. After a short and one-sided engagement, she was scuttled by her own crew.

▲
SMS *Dresden* in Scapa Flow (Imperial War Museum)

Because of this, *Dresden* could not join the fleet as an active and fully operational unit until August, 1918, when she was assigned to the Second Scouting Group in company with *Karlsruhe, Königsberg* and *Emden.*

The ship's main armament was similar to that of *Köln*, with the 5·9-inch guns mounted in all the same dispositions with the exception of the two guns mounted to port and starboard and abeam of the bridge. On *Dresden*, these were mounted a deck lower than on *Köln*. The hull sides at upper deck level were cut back at the after ends of the forecastle and the guns were mounted on the external platforms formed. These were precariously small, making the manning of the guns dangerous in a heavy sea. (It is difficult to understand why *Dresden* was so designed — by this time all ships' guns in other navies were being mounted as high as practicable away from heavy seas and to afford as high a vantage point as possible.)

Dresden could carry 120 mines on the after end of the upper deck, which were launched from the stern in the same way as in the *Königsberg II*-class ships. Officers' accommodation was distributed in a similar manner to those ships, and the deckhouses comprising the after superstructure were used, together with areas of the middle deck below the mine storage facilities. The senior officers' wardroom was halfway along the starboard side of the after deckhouse. The remainder of the space within this structure was taken up with cabins and bathrooms, with the more junior officers' wardroom situated on the forward starboard side.

Machinery spaces were provided below the middle deck, where boiler rooms comprised most of the length of the hull. Turbine rooms were situated aft of these with generator rooms and hydraulic pump rooms further aft and beneath the middle deck. There were magazines and shell rooms on the platform deck before the after gun emplacement and the hydraulic system for the steering gear was in the stern. Forward of the boiler rooms were diesel generator rooms, used when the boilers were shut down, and forward again were magazines for the forward guns. Further forward, the lower deck spaces were taken up with storerooms, lamp rooms and anchor chain lockers. The crews' accommodation was above these within the forecastle. It was subdivided longitudinally to separate the seamen and stokers from the non-commissioned officers. There was further sub-division forward into rooms for specialist equipment for mines and gun maintenance. Storage rooms were also provided for the mens' hammocks, about 200 of which had to be folded and packed away at each watch.

Electric power was used for everything from cooking to operating the engine and boiler room telegraphs. Accommodation areas were heated by electric radiators which must have made considerable demands on the generators in cold weather. They must have been welcome, however, inside the bare steel bulkheads and hull sides of the ship where inflammable materials were, wisely, virtually non-existent. Using 220v DC power and lead-covered cables, condensation within the hull would have added to the normal problems of electricity at sea — a nightmare for the electrical engineers on the ships. The clearing of earth faults probably took up the most time, and the complexities of fittings designed to eliminate ingress of water made tasks as simple as changing light bulbs more than five minute jobs.

The *Dresden*-class cruisers were fitted with 8 coal and 6 oil-fired boilers supplying steam to two geared turbines. Cruising range was increased over the previous class of German cruisers by 600 miles, to 5,400 miles, but the only two completed ships of the class were commissioned too late in the conflict to take advantage of this. While Germany had ample supplies of coal for her warships, oil was only available from the limited oilfields of central Europe. (Britain had access to her Middle East oilfields, but were initially wary of solely oil-powered ships in case enemy action deprived them of these.)

Dresden's armour protection comprised a citadel within the ship, (which was accepted warship design by this time). Behind the 2½-inch armour plate of the hull side, (which extended for about ⅔ of the ship,) were the almost mandatory wing coal bunkers. The middle deck was also the armoured deck, and was of ¾-inch steel sloping downwards slightly above the wing coal bunkers to join the exterior armour. Thus the citadel was formed, closed by an armour steel collision bulkhead forward and extending aft to enclose the vital steering gear and after 5·9-inch gun magazines. The conning tower, as the nerve centre of the ship, was protected by 4-inch armour plate steel.

The German light cruisers, like the larger battleships and battlecruisers, were remarkably well-built. Sub-division into many water-tight compartments, with excellent damage-control arrangements coupled with well-practised operating techniques, ensured their resistance to sinking. The bulkheads between compartments below the waterline were completely sealed. No doors were fitted and no pipes, electrical cables or ducting passed through them, thus ensuring great watertight integrity. (This was well-demonstrated at Jutland when *Wiesbaden* was struck by innumerable British shells, but stubbornly remained afloat.) During preparations for scuttling the light cruisers at Scapa Flow, their crews had drilled holes through these bulkheads to ensure adequate flooding. Despite these desperate measures, the tiny British guard force managed to save three light cruisers, and others took as long as four hours to settle following their immolation.

From her joining the Fleet until 7th November, 1918,

Dresden's commander was Korvettenkapitän Prinz von Preussen of the German nobility. Under his command, she took on board a full load of mines in August, to be laid to the west of the mouth of the Ems River, (to protect the port of Emden from possible British attack). Existing minefields had to be frequently supplemented in case enemy intelligence had learnt of their limits, or even more dangerous, had located the safe channels through them. While on this mission, *Dresden* was torpedoed by a British submarine, causing flooding of some boiler rooms and damage to a turbine. Her sub-division and damage control arrangments coped with the flooding, and escorted by torpedo boat destroyers, she limped back to harbour for extensive repairs. Doubtless she never would have survived to sail to Scapa Flow but for the presence of the destroyers who forced the submarines to submerge and retire.

Following the dispersal of the Fleet, (after mutiny had prevented the intended sortie at the end of October,) *Dresden* sailed to Swinemunde on the Baltic north coast of Germany. In the deep water anchorage for the port of Stettin, her commander lowered his flag on November 7th. For the following week she was under the command of Kapitän zur See Frank, who in turn handed her over to Kapitänleutnant Fabricius who had volunteered to take her into internment. *Dresden* was unable to join the assembled internment fleet on the 19th November due to a turbine failure and still uncompleted repairs. She did not arrive at Scapa Flow until December 6th, when she sailed through Hoxa Sound with *König* and the Torpedo Boat Destroyer *V129*, (sent as replacement for *V30* which struck a mine and sank at the start of the main part of the Fleet's voyage).

Dresden dropped anchor for the last time off the east shore of Cava, some three cables to the east of *König* and with a splendid view of the British Fleet's main anchorage off Flotta. It is doubtful whether the crew left to man *Dresden* appreciated this, cold and poorly-nourished during the winter months and confined on their rat-infested, inhospitable ship. On the 21st June, 1919, her crew took to their boats as Orkney sea water poured into the stricken shp. A drifter assigned to guard the fleet secured lines to her and struggled to drag the stubborn, waterlogged bulk into the shallow waters off Cava, but *Dresden* won the battle when at 13.30 she finally capsized to port to disappear amidst gushes of air and spray.

┌─*Diving on DRESDEN*──────

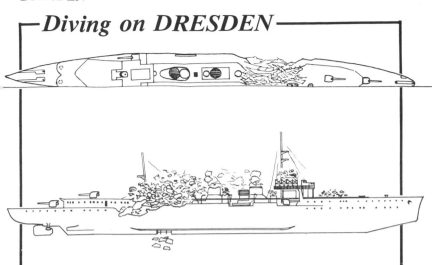

As patches of oil spread across the surface to mark where
she lay, *Dresden* settled in 33-36 metres of water in position
N 58° 52' 59", W 03° 18' 22" — a tragic waste of a fine,
almost new, example of fighting ship. It is not surprising
that the French were so angry at the loss of these ships
which were more than a match for the equivalent ship of
any navy. At the same time, a great sigh of relief must
have been heard from the British Admiralty building in
Whitehall.

Untouched, but no doubt surveyed by both Cox and
Danks and Metal Industries after the Second World War,
Dresden was leased by Nundy Salvage, then by Clark
Diving Services. Neither exploited the wreck to its full
potential, and the ship still provides a magnificent spectacle
to the diver, being almost intact and covered in particularly
dense marine growth. A bell was recovered from *Dresden*
in 1980 by amateur divers from West Riding Sub-Aqua
Club, and this is amongst the display of artefacts from the
German Fleet at the Stromness Museum, (a short walk up
Victoria Street from Stromness harbour). The display is an
interesting diversion between dives for those who wish to
improve their knowledge of the scuttling and salvaging of
the German Fleet.

The divers fin hard down the line landing heavily on
the wreck, and then fin down the hull to the keel as the
hull curves down until vertical. They land on the seabed at
34 metres, where it is darker now in the shadow of
Dresden's looming hull.

Hull plates missing from the ship's bottom lie on the

seabed, and the hole left exposes voids which were oil or
water storage compartments within the ship's double
bottom. Finning to the left, along the seabed with the now
intact hull above, (noticing the odd scallop and crab,) they
soon arrive at the rudder lying flat on the seabed. *Dresden*
is now recognised as lying on her port side as they fin
round the curve of the stern, passing the stern anchor still
in its hawse. They move round the hull edge to the
quarterdeck, rising vertically from the stones and shale of
the bottom. Set into the timber deck planking is an open
square hatch, (in fact a rotted deck light,) but fallen
steelwork inside blocks access into the officers'
accommodation area. Finning forward to the aftermost gun
mounted at the forward end of the quarterdeck, the divers
move around to the open breech inside the protective
shield. Torchlight picks out the recoil cylinder and some
gun operating handwheels, now partly camouflaged by
marine growth. There is easy access to the officers' quarters
through the space where the after bulkhead of the
deckhouse once was.

Finning inside to the Commanding Officer's quarters,
(past the aftermost gun's flashguard extending from the
superstructure deck to the left,) there is lead-covered wiring
draped between brass lamps. (All the lamps have broken
glasses, and some hang from the wiring detached from
corroded mountings.) Debris litters the bottom. There are
collapsed bulkheads, remains of heaters and a full-size
bath. (The white porcelain stands out against the silt and
rust flakes.) Finning forward through holes in wasted
bulkheads, squeezing between support frames and dodging
beneath hanging cables, the divers reach the barbette of the
after superimposed 5·9-inch gun, with electric motors and
gearboxes which operated the training mechanism and
ammunition hoists. Passing above this, light from above
contrasts with the total blackness ahead. There is an access
door in the starboard bulkhead above, which leads to the
outside of the deckhouse side, with the starboard deck on
the right.

Finning forward along the deck, with the shuttered
square windows in the deckhouse side below them, the
intact hull gives way to buckled and distorted plating where
salvage work has taken place. After passing hanging deck
frames, collapsed and buckled plates and bent pipes, the
ship again assumes recognisable form. A boiler room
ventilator is passed — a large structure with louvred slate.
Heavy, curved boat davits hang overhead and bent funnel

plating lies below on the seabed. Further up the wreck, past the shell of a torpedo launcher on the starboard weatherdeck, is the breech end of the starboard forward wing 5·9-inch gun, neatly fitting into the cut-away in the hull side. The platform space opens onto the weatherdeck inboard of the gun. The weapon appears to be intact except for the missing breech closing wedge and sights, and the open barrel points dead ahead, no tompion in place. Finning away from the wreck, the divers drop down to land on the side of the bridge structure. Steel rigging ropes drape across bent handrails, which lead to the conning tower just below, almost on the seabed. The access door is tight on the shale-covered bottom, and forward the command bridge is open and empty. Not so many years ago the glass was still intact.

Dropping to the seabed once more, the divers fin forward, with the forecastle deck to their right rising high above and reducing light. A large hole in the deck gives easy access to the forecastle and the small galley built into the trunking below the conning tower. Through the open door is a stack of rusting enamel mugs. Forward, missing hull plates in the starboard side provide an exit, and the divers land back on the seabed amongst bent and flimsy plating, the remains of hatch weather shields and ammunition lockers. Forward are the empty mountings for the forward 5·9-inch guns, which are now missing.

Forward again, the hull profile begins to taper towards the bow. The port bulwark emerges from the silty bottom and gently sweeps up towards the point of the prow, which is now some five metres above. The gradual sweep of the bow is silhouetted against the lights from above and the starboard anchor chain drapes over the curve and falls to the seabed close by. The studded links disappear, sunk into the shells and small stones of the bottom. The British drifter could not have moved *Dresden* very far in her attempts to beach her!

There are heavy fairleads on the prow for mooring and towing ropes beneath a dense growth of tiny anemones. (The shining pink, vivid red and yellow can be exploited by torchlight.) Along from the sharp bow entry is the forefoot, and turning right, the divers fin aft where the bow angles down to the keel. Continuing aft gives little reward as the hull plating is intact, interrupted only by grilles. Finning up over the bilge keel and along the flat hull side, the divers arrive back at the starboard wing gun to ascend. And so they return to the dive boat to compare notes about their dive on this magnificent wreck.

Chapter 9
OTHER SITES OF INTEREST

V83

THE UNDERWATER MINE was developed into a formidable and highly effective weapon by many countries who relied on their naval power for their defence. The idea, however, of a propelled underwater weapon which could be used against stronger naval forces had immense appeal, as such a weapon could be more effective in offence than the static mine. During the latter half of the last century, many odd designs were tried, tested and failed, but the Whitehead torpedo finally became the ultimate solution. This long, lean fish-like device carried an explosive warhead and was driven by a compressed air-powered reciprocating engine which turned a pair of contra-rotating propellers. Direction and depth were controlled by a small gyro unit which operated diminutive rudders fitted to the trailing edges of fins at the tail. The torpedo could be launched from a tube mounted on a ship's deck, ejected by compressed air; and the compressed air capacity within the torpedo could power the earliest designs for a distance of about six hundred yards.

In this awesome new weapon, those nations with small navies could counter effectively the massive fleets maintained by more powerful countries. Germany, after purchasing some Whitehead torpedoes in 1882, began constructing small, fast torpedo boats to carry them. They were to attack at night, launching their weapons under the cover of darkness and escape before being caught. Britain had already commissioned some, and in anticipation, had also fitted their larger ships with secondary armament to fend off an enemy's torpedo boats.

▲
F2
(Author's
collection)

74

Britain also developed another type of larger craft, which carried guns of greater range and power than the three or four pounders mounted on torpedo boats, and which themselves carried torpedo tubes. They could thus catch and destroy enemy torpedo boats, sail with the fleet to protect the big ships from them and yet use torpedoes in the same way.

Until late in the war, German torpedo boats were, generally speaking, smaller than the British destroyers. Although fitted with similar surface armament, the German ships carried more torpedo tubes and were more akin to the orginal torpedo boats than the British model. The German ships were also painted black for night attack, but they too became fleet vessels and were used in a similar manner to British destroyers.

Until 1915, only three German shipyards built torpedo boat destroyers: the Schichau yard at Elbing, whose products were given the prefix 'S'; Krupp's Germaniawerft yard at Kiel, whose boats were prefixed 'G'; and the Vulcan yard at Stettin whose boats were prefixed 'V'. The German torpedo boats were given numbers, not names, and those were consecutive. Thus in 1912, Vulcan built the class *V1* to *V6*. Germaniawerft built another type designated *G7* to *G12*, and Schichau yet another type numbered *S13* to *S24*, and so on. Original German torpedo boats from 1899 had been similarly numbered, but with the commencement of the new series of ships in 1912, those were re-christened with the new prefix 'T'. Germany had some 107 'T' boats, mostly smaller than the later series of vessels, with only three or four torpedo tubes.

Beginning with the *V1* of 1912, German torpedo boats grew increasingly larger with each class. While the *V1*-class were 225 feet long with a displacement of 697 tons, the *V67*-class, of which *V83* was one, had grown to 269 feet long with a beam of 27½ feet and a displacement of 1,118 tons. The ultimate German torpedo boat, the flotilla leader *S113* of 1918, had grown to 2,400 tons on a length of 338 feet — almost a light cruiser!

V83 joined the Fleet on 5th July, 1916, only days too late to participate at the Battle of Jutland. Powered by twin geared turbines driving two screws, she was capable of a little over 36 knots. She carried three 4·1-inch guns in single unprotected mountings and six 50cm torpedo tubes. Two of these were forward of the bridge and behind the forecastle each singly mounted, a pair were in a twin mounting aft of the aftermost funnel, and another pair together forward of the mainmast. In addition, *V83* could carry 24 mines on deck — a versatile and lethal mixture — and she required a crew of about 100. On joining the Fleet she was attached to the 7th Destroyer Flotilla, and her time was spent variously on routine patrols off Heligoland, battle tactics practices in the Baltic, and detachment to Zeebrugge from where they could launch night attacks on British shipping in the English Channel. This included attacks on the trawlers and drifters which watched over the anti U-boat defences designed to prevent those boats from penetrating the Channel area.

Diving on V83

On her scuttling, a Royal Navy party managed to beach the ship on the east shore of Rysa Little, where she lies with her bow in 5-8 metres and her stern in 11-14 metres. Only her stern remains intact, upright and balanced on the propeller shaft bearing brackets. The forward two thirds of the hull are broken up and lie on a rock shelf covered with a thick growth of kelp. All manner of wreckage is beneath the kelp, from portholes to copper aerial rigging screws, flat plates, chains, hawsers and pipes. On the after deck is a 4·1-inch gun, almost hidden beneath kelp and sponges, with another lying on the rock further forward, off the port side of the wreck. The tubular steel propeller guards protrude from the hull side aft, and the rudder stands intact beneath the stern overhang. The propeller shaft sternmost bearings are on the sandy seabed further forward. A hole above the starboard propeller guard affords access to the stern section, which has no fittings and only a few deck support columns. Rooting around in the silt on the deck has turned up an occasional signal shell — (they were used on one interned boat to clean the wardroom coal-fired stove flue, until one broke out of the corroded pipe to fizz and burn around the wardroom as the officers scrambled to safety)!

Exit from the stern can be made after finning forward between the support columns to emerge amongst the kelp growing thickly from the rock shelf, (often surprising one of the larger wrasse found feeding around the wreck). Finning aft round the stern, the kedge anchor is still in place, and then forward along the port side to the rock shelf, the diver can root amongst the thick laminaria stalks for whatever might be found amongst the tangled wreckage. *V83* makes for a relaxing, easy dive after having been on one of the deep wrecks.

BREMSE

Built at the Vulcan Yard in Stettin, *Bremse* was identical to her sister *Brummer*, but was launched some four months later. The most documented action in which she was involved is recorded in the chapter on *Brummer*. Other than that, her duties appear to have been confined to occasional mine-laying sorties off Germany's North Sea bases. On her scuttling she was almost beached by the Royal Navy on the foreshore off Toy Ness, (to the west of Swanbister Bay in the north of Scapa Flow,) where she finally foundered and turned onto her starboard side as she sank. The wreck lay on a slope, with her bow and part of her port side exposed at low water, until 1929 when Cox and Danks began salvage work on her. Immense difficulties were caused by fuel oil from the ship's double bottom tanks spilling through the ship, which had to be turned completely upside down before lifting the hull could begin. This was finally achieved after the superstructure had been removed, and the leaking hull was taken to Lyness for breaking as it was not considered feasible to tow it as far as Rosyth.

Diving on BREMSE

The remains of the superstructure are located by first finding a pair of anchor chains running up the stony foreshore at Toy Ness, (presumably used to secure the hull during salvage attempts). About thirty yards offshore from these, in only 7-10 metres of water, are some flat plates and deck support beams from the superstructure and foredeck of *Bremse*. An anchor capstan drive gear, with drive clutch assembly and anti-fall back ratchet wheel still attached, lies adjacent to and in the midst of drive shafts and piping, surrounded by masses of *Chorda filum* (Dead Men's Ropes). A little further offshore, the forward 5.9-inch gun of *Bremse* is lying on one side, the mounting pedestal sheared off at its base. Deeper and just to the west of the gun, the distorted remains of a part of the superstructure lies on the seabed. Inside are such relics as a toilet, hydraulic pipes and associated fittings, some small lamps — perhaps indicator lamps of some description — and many electrical fittings. A mast lies further south, which is as far as the author has ever ventured. No doubt much more of the top hamper of *Bremse* lies further south, and must be worth further investigation.

UB 116

From the German side the war was lost by October 25th, 1918, when the small coastal U-boat, *UB-116*, set sail for Scapa Flow to penetrate the harbour's defences and torpedo any British ships inside. Her commanding officer, Lieutenant J. J. Emsmann, had been advised by the Commander of U-boats, Commodore Michelson, that Hoxa Sound to the south of Scapa Flow could be forced by a small U-boat, submerged and under the cover of night. Because this was the main passage for the Grand Fleet, Hoxa Sound was not thought to be mined or protected by boom defence nets. In fact, it was well protected; underwater hydrophones could pick up the engine and propeller noises of a submerged U-boat; looped cables detected the change in the earth's magnetic field caused by a steel hull passing over them; and mines near the bottom of Hoxa Sound could be electrically detonated from a hut ashore. Should all these fail there was a boom defence net across the deep entrance tended by drifters, and searchlights were mounted ashore to sweep the surface during the hours of darkness. *UB-116* had an impossible task before her.

At 20.21 on October 28th, the listeners ashore heard through the hydrophones the sounds of an unscheduled vessel approaching. The searchlights were switched on, and at 22.30, a periscope was seen to break surface briefly. Only minutes later, the U-boat was passing over the mines. These were instantly detonated, and a large patch of oil on the surface proved that *UB-116* was no longer any threat.

The wreck of the U-boat was raised in 1919, but foundered again further into Hoxa Sound, off the east coast of Flotta in the entrance to Pan Hope Bay, where she now lies. In 1969 she was sold for salvage, but time had taken its toll and instead of attempting to lift her in one piece, explosives were used to break her up into smaller pieces. In the process, the existence of live torpedoes inside was supposedly overlooked. (Unconfirmed reports state that one or more detonated, breaking up the U-boat considerably more than was intended.) At the time, however, oil was being found in large quantities in the North Sea, and the oil companies were looking for convenient places to pipe their black gold ashore for refining. Orkney was ideal for such an operation, but a U-boat full of deteriorating torpedoes could pose a threat to any seabed pipeline, and had to be got rid of. What could be more expedient than to use her own weapons?

The impression of the wreck today is that all ten of her torpedoes blew up as her remains are spread over quite a wide area. Nothing even suggests that this was once an *Unterseeboote*.

Pipes, twisted steel plates, wires and broken remains of

switchboxes are all that remain of *UB-116*, unwittingly sent out on a suicide mission — the last defiant gesture of the Kaiserliche Marine.

F2

This World War II ship was one of a type classed as 'Geleiteboote' ('escort boat'), which were similar to the corvettes built by the Allies — anti-submarine vessels to be used as killer-hunters to protect both merchant and warships. They were a relatively new concept for the Reichsmarine and to some extent were experimental ships. Their machinery and equipment were complex for such small vessels and unreliable.

They were similar in size to World War I torpedo boats, *F2* being 260 feet long with a beam of 29 feet, driven by turbines geared to two shafts. She carried two 105mm single guns on shielded pedestal mountings, (one on her forecastle deck and one on her superstructure deck aft,) and an assortment of anti-aircraft armament. At the end of the Second World War, *F2* was handed over to Britain as war reparations, and moored in Gutter Sound north of Lyness. She lay there for some months, until, on December 30th, 1946, she foundered during a gale, believed to have sprung a severe leak. Evidently she was not considered worth lifting and was left until 1968 when she was sold for salvage.

Diving on F2

She lies in position N 58° 50′ 46″; W 03° 11′ 30″ where the seabed depth is 16 metres at high water. Her wreck is marked by a red can buoy as her bulk rises to within 7 metres of the surface. Her stern stands upright supported on the propeller shaft bearing brackets, but her hull is broken in half and the forepart rests on its port side. The forward gun is intact and her starboard anchor chain leads out from her bow. Her single mast lies flat on the seabed, the searchlight platform the only recognisable part of it. A barge lies close by full of bits and pieces salvaged from her wreck. On 15th November, 1968, this was moored alongside while pieces of *F2* were raised and taken on board. A gale that night sent the salvaged bits of *F2* back to the seabed, this time in the barge, and they have remained there since.

Diving in the 'Foul Ground' Areas

The battlecruisers *Seydlitz, Moltke* and *von der Tann,* together with the *Kaiser*-class battleships, *Kaiser* and *Prinzregent Luitpold,* were all scuttled to the east along the channel between Cava and Green Head on Hoy. On the Admiralty Chart of the area, 'Foul Ground' is marked along almost the whole length of the Cava side of this channel. Diving almost anywhere here brings various rewards. A funnel casing filled with concrete, and further weighted with the bower and sheet anchors of one of the capital ships, was perhaps used to help stabilise one of the hulks during salvage. Not far off lies an 3.4-inch gun complete with protective shield, and even the remains of a simple sight. In the distance, past some heavy hawsers, is another 3.4-inch gun, this one with its barrel broken and shield missing. In another area, an almost complete conning tower lies upside down and partly buried into the seabed. A door in its side, partly hidden beneath the overhanging bridge wing, gives access into a control room, the bulkheads covered with electrical switch and fuse boxes. The author has seen photographs of two sextants recovered from this room.

To the north of Gutter Sound lay the *Kaiser*-class battleship *Kaiserin*, in position **N 58° 53' 20"; W 03° 11' 48"**, in a general depth of 42 metres. She was lifted by Metal Industries Ltd. in 1936, and after her superstructure had been blasted away in shallower water close to Lyness, she was towed to Rosyth for demolition.

As the vessel sank she turned over to port, her masts shearing off at superstructure deck level. Her motor boats fixed to the superstructure deck were crushed under the massive 24,000 ton weight as she settled into the seabed. Not much now remains of *Kaiserin*. Two diesel engines from the motor boats lie about 40 feet apart and there are pieces of hull timbers, small boilers and engine room fittings from the boats. A small steam windlass from the launch, lies some way ahead of one engine, and not far away lie the broken masts of *Kaiserin*. The mainmast searchlight platform survives intact complete with switch boxes and the remains of telephones. Wire hawsers and pieces of plate and teak lie about the seabed, together with the occasional length of heavy, brass flexible pipe left by Metal Industries. Massive craters in the seabed remain, where gun turrets and conning towers were deep in the sediment. One is almost 50 metres, this left by the forward conning tower and bridge structure. The area cannot be adequately covered in one dive, and much must remain for future discovery.

In shallow water not far from Lyness, a bell from the battleship *Friedrich der Grosse,* (Flagship of the Fleet at Jutland,) was found and raised by members of the Golden Lion Sub-Aqua Club from Wrexham in 1984. This now resides in the Stromness Museum. And so will the story continue. As long as people are inquisitive, and divers still visit these sites, so more will be unearthed for future generations to be reminded of a previous great arms race, which ultimately led to the destruction of an empire, and the division of the nation which dared to challenge it.

The old axiom that 'there is nothing new under the sun', was refuted by the ships of the Great War, whose ultimate demise as a class was only the result of further technological development. During the Second World War, the weakness of these still magnificent fighting ships was amply demonstrated by the sinking of the old British battleship, HMS *Royal Oak.* Germany's ultimate battleship, *Bismarck*, was sunk a little over a year later after being crippled by torpedoes from British aircraft. The final humiliation for the battleship, however, was the easy sinking of HMS *Prince of Wales*, along with the elderly but efficient battlecruiser, HMS *Repulse*, by Japanese torpedoes. Their day was done, but what a pity none has survived. The last true Dreadnought from the Great War was HMS *Canada*, which had fought at Jutland in 1916. She was sold to Chile in 1920 for whom she had been originally built, and was re-named *Almirante Latorre*, being finally broken up in Japan in 1959. Her destruction brought to a final close the era of the Dreadnought battleship, and only the wrecks at Scapa Flow remain as the final monuments to their class, and to the Great War at Sea.

Chapter 10
DISASTER AT SCAPA FLOW

AFTER BRITAIN had taken the naval world by storm in 1906 with the commissioning of the all-powerful battleship, HMS *Dreadnought*, her priority was to keep ahead of the world's naval powers by building more vessels faster than any other nation. Even while *Dreadnought* was building, designs were under way for three more of her type — improvements on *Dreadnought* and designated *Bellerophon* class. Work had hardly begun on those when the next three keels were being laid for the third group; the *St Vincent* class. They were to be similar to the *Bellerophons* but slightly longer and wider, with more powerful machinery to compensate for the additional displacement. They were also fitted with a new type of 12-inch gun which had greater muzzle velocity than the earlier model and could hit more distant targets. The first of the three ships to commission was HMS *Vanguard* in February 1910, and she was the first Dreadnought battleship to be built at the Vickers Shipyard, Barrow-in-Furness.

For her main armament *Vanguard* carried ten 12-inch/50 calibre guns mounted in twin gunned turrets. Three were arranged along the ship's centreline, and one each to port and starboard between the funnels. *Vanguard* and her predecessors could therefore fire an 8-gun broadside from their main armament. Unlike the German ships, power for all the turret functions — training, elevation, gun run-out and ammunition hoists — was hydraulic, pressure being generated by steam pumps and piped to the individual turrets. The rammers for shells and charges were mounted on the gun breeches which enabled loading the gun at any angle of elevation, and, theoretically, should have contributed to a higher rate of fire than the German ships. In practice there was little difference, and the British 12-inch Mk XI gun, as fitted to *Vanguard* and other battleships, proved to be less accurate than both the predecessing 12-inch/45 calibre guns and the larger calibre armament developed for later British capital ships.

Propelled by two sets of Parsons reaction marine turbines directly driving four propeller shafts, she could attain 21 knots, (decided upon by naval tacticians as the maximum speed of the Fleet in deployment). Power for the turbines was generated from 18 large tube boilers working at 250 psi, principally coal-fired but fitted with supplementary oil burners. This complex machinery provided 24,500 s.h.p. Although one of the most sophisticated floating machines of the time, she was soon to be superseded by even more complex and efficient ships. The five years following *Vanguard's* building saw advances in warship and armament design previously unparalleled.

The hull side armour belt of *Vanguard* was, at its maximum, 10 inches thick, but only extended down from main deck level, one deck above the waterline, (except over the wing 12-inch gun barbettes where the plating rose up to the upper deck to protect the wing turret magazines). The horizontal armoured deck within the hull was three inches thick. The armour plate itself was a high tensile alloy steel containing nickel, chromium, manganese and vanadium.

Following her trials and working up period, *Vanguard* joined the First Division of the Home Fleet. She practised tactical manoeuvres and exercises from her base at Chatham with other units of the Fleet for two years. In 1912, the Fleet was reorganised into squadrons and *Vanguard* joined the First Battle Squadron as Flagship for a period. When war broke out she was a private ship, carrying no rear-admiral, and a unit of the Fourth Division of the Fourth Battle Squadron of the Grand Fleet.

Vanguard spent most of her time at Scapa Flow, with frequent sweeps across the North Sea to either lure out the High Seas Fleet or give chase after the raids on England's east coast. During the long periods spent at anchor, the crews of the British ships were kept fully occupied, not only by coaling, provisioning, cleaning and maintaining their vessels, but inter-ship football, boxing and athletics competitions were organised on Flotta and at Lyness. (A golf course was laid out on Flotta and ships' crews even tended their own gardens ashore at Crockness on the north side of Longhope Bay.)

At the Battle of Jutland (the only time her guns were fired in anger,) *Vanguard* was 16th ship in the line of Jellicoe's 24 Dreadnoughts facing the Germans at the end of the northwards chase. Some on board *Vanguard* witnessed the destruction of HMS *Defence* which blew up as her magazines were ignited by German shells which exploded inside the ship. (It was as well that those on *Vanguard* knew nothing of what fate held in store for her.) *Vanguard* opened fire on the German light cruiser SMS *Wiesbaden*, and reported her as disabled. At the end of the fighting, *Vanguard* had fired eighty 12-inch shells and ten 4-inch, and had contributed to sinking *Wiesbaden* and fending off attacking torpedo boats. She had come through the fight completely unscathed and was ready for action the following morning, although the Germans had reached safety during the hours of darkness. The Battle Fleet set course for Scapa Flow, there being nothing more to do.

The pattern of operations for the Grand Fleet during the following year was much as it had been before. Jellicoe was recalled to the Admiralty in November 1916, to become Second Sea Lord, and was replaced by Admiral Sir David Beatty, He continued the frequent sweeps across the North Sea, but only twice between June 1916 and October 1918 was the Grand Fleet to steam out of Scapa Flow knowing that the High Seas Fleet had left its bases, and both times the Germans avoided confrontation. When the two Fleets finally met again on 21st November, 1918, *Vanguard* was not among the British ships, her end having come over a year before in horrific, if spectacular, circumstances.

When the Fleet was at Scapa Flow, the capital ships were moored in parallel lines off the north shore of Flotta. On July 9th, 1917, *Vanguard* had been carrying out exercises in the north of Scapa Flow and returned to her position in the 4th Squadron in the late afternoon. During the early evening, a number of her officers left the ship to attend a concert being held on board HMS *Royal Oak*. All was calm and serene until 23.20, when, in the pale light of the Orkney summer nights, a sheet of bright orange flame shot high into the air from aft of *Vanguard's* foremast. After a second or two, this sudden, frightening column of flame developed into a great mountain of vivid light which illuminated the whole Fleet and darkened the sky. Then, a colossal, numbing explosion extinguished the flame, and *Vanguard* was lost to sight in a black cloud of smoke, and bits of her began to rain down on the Fleet. A complete 12-inch gun turret, weighing over 400 tons, landed on Flotta almost a mile away from the ship, and burning debris set fire to the moorland. The crews of the other ships threw burning wreckage of the battleship overboard before it ignited their own ammunition, and boats set out to search for survivors. Only three were found, one of whom died later from his injuries. Although 24 officers and 71 men had not been on board at the time, 804 had still perished in that devastating inferno.

All manner of items were salvaged from the wreckage which floated among the fleet or was washed up on the surrounding islands — gruesome human remains, ropes, fenders, hammocks and even the ship's 50-foot steam pinnace, virtually intact. Also found were letters written in German, a German edition of the Bible and a photograph of a pretty young lady with a German inscription. News of these findings quickly spread through the fleet, and many concluded that *Vanguard* was lost due to sabotage by an enemy agent. To further embellish the idea, it was discovered at the Court of Inquiry that a civilian ordnance fitter, who had left *Vanguard* only hours before she blew up, had also been working on the cruiser HMS *Natal* before that ship was lost at Cromarty Firth in almost identical circumstances in 1915. This man, together with the German letters and photograph were passed to Naval Intelligence for further examination. After investigating the systems on *Vanguard* for checking magazine temperatures, (which surprisingly was not standard procedure,) and considering problems which could cause dramatic temperature rises in magazines, the Court of Inquiry concluded that she could have blown up as the result of spontaneous ignition of either unstable cordite or abnormal deterioration of ageing cordite. They did not, however, totally discount the possibility of sabotage. The author A. Cecil Hampshire, in his book 'They Called it Accident', advises that the ordnance fitter returned to his duties after interrogation by Naval Intelligence, who found nothing wrong with his conduct.

With regard to the German letters, photograph and Bible, it is possible that there was a perfectly innocent explanation. Only five weeks before war broke out, British warships had paid a courtesy visit to Kiel to attend the re-opening of the Kiel-Wilhelmshaven Canal after it had been closed for widening. It is conceivable that relationships were struck between some British sailors and German women, and that these finds were mementoes, the sailor involved having been, unluckily, subsequently transferred to *Vanguard*.

Since that dreadful July night, *Vanguard*, or what was left of her, has remained rusting under the waters of Scapa Flow. Nundy Marine Metals were granted a licence to salvage the wreck during the 1960s and '70s, and spasmodic work was carried out. Because of this, it is now impossible to know how much of *Vanguard* remained after the accident. Her stern now lies about 70 degrees to port, 60 feet or so of it intact, with a solitary 3-pounder signal gun standing guard over the crazily-angled teak planking of the quarterdeck, (still white beneath the accumulated sediment). The rudder remains in place on the other side of the stern section and anti-torpedo netting lies just off the wreckage on the seabed.

Forward of the break in the hull, at the termination of the stern section, the seabed is littered with wreckage. Slender rods of cordite are scattered all around, and among twisted and tangled steel plates lies a 12-inch gun burnt off about 30 feet from the breech with a heavy lifting chain wrapped around it. Forward of this stands the barbette of the aftermost 12-inch gun emplacement. In British ships the main gun turrets were designated letters of the alphabet, and on *Vanguard* and similar ships, 'A' was the foremost turret, 'P' and 'Q' the port and starboard midships' turrets, 'X' the next moving aft and 'Y' the aftermost. 'Y' barbette now stands as high as the turret roller ring track — some slewing rollers are still in place but there is no sign of the turret. Whether this was blown off or was salvaged for the value of its steel remains a mystery. Forward of the barbette the wreckage becomes isolated pieces of distorted hull and superstructure, among which lie occasional shards of broken crockery and an odd boot — pathetic reminders of the fate of most of her crew. About 80 feet of the ship's bow remains intact, standing with a slight port list with the deck sloping aft almost to the seabed. The bottom is blown out where 'A' turret magazines would have been. The glass in the bow scuttles is either missing completely, or starred by the shock of the explosion, and the hull plating at the break in the hull is cut clean off but bent outwards at the edges. Proof, if any were needed, that the ship blew up from inside.

The foredeck planking remains intact and anchor cables are still held in their slips; even the foredeck hatch weathershield remains in place. This is the final resting place of many who died so tragically in the disaster, and no diver of principle would enter the hull in this section. Standing on the seabed at the foot of the ram-shaped stem and looking up the fine lines of the bow towering 50 feet above the diver, there is no more majestic and befitting memorial to those men, the cause of whose demise still remains something of a mystery. Salvage rights to the wreck finally expired in 1982, and it was declared a war grave, banned to divers in 1983. Prosecution faces anyone attempting to dive her today.

The Court of Inquiry never seriously considered that *Vanguard* had been sunk by a U-boat, and there may have been good reason for this. When Jellicoe assumed command of the Grand Fleet on August 4th, 1914, he had already found Scapa Flow's defences against U-boats inadequate and had requested action from the Admiralty. At that time it was believed that the strength of the tide races between the islands surrounding the anchorage was sufficient to exclude access to these craft, (and it was doubted that they possessed sufficient operating range to reach Scapa Flow). As early in the war as August 9th, 1914, however, the cruiser HMS *Birmingham* rammed and sank the German *U-15* off Fair Isle. After this, constant look-outs were maintained on all ships in Scapa Flow for sightings of marauding U-boats. After a number of false alarms had unnerved the whole fleet, they left Scapa Flow for temporary bases, less convenient but believed to be more secure.

Meanwhile, the Admiralty made urgent plans for closing the gaps between the islands in Scapa Flow. Nets were fitted across the main entrances to the Flow, and merchant ships were sunk in the narrow channels used only by small local craft, principally fishing boats. The deepest of these narrows was Skerry Sound (between the tiny islands of Lamb Holm and Glims Holm in the north east of Scapa Flow,) which, at 40 feet deep and almost 300 yards wide, could have allowed through a semi-submerged U-boat. Seven ships were scuttled across this entrance, and by February, 1915, Skerry Sound was effectively closed to all shipping. On the 14th September, the 30-feet deep East Weddel Sound between Glims Holm and Burray was also closed by sinking three ships across its 200 yard-wide channel. The shallower water sound between Burray and South Ronaldsay, (the narrowest of the eastern channels at about 150 yards,) was considered closed with the sinking of a single ship, SS *Lorne*.

To the west of Scapa Flow, six ships were sunk across the fast-flowing waters of Burra Sound, (between the islands of Graemsay and Hoy,) which was 30 feet deep at high water and 200 yards wide. One of the ships, the *Gobernador Bories*, is still an interesting and popular dive, although only possible at slack water.

One more entrance to Scapa Flow remained open — the most northerly of the eastern channels, Kirk Sound, which was the 430 yard stretch between mainland Orkney and the tiny Lamb Holm. The Sound, (about 30 feet deep at high water,) was effectively blocked by four ships from the north: *Numidian, Aorangi, Minieh* and *Thames*.

Scapa Flow was considered to be reasonably secure by November 5th, 1914, and the Grand Fleet returned. The anchorage was only empty during the next four years when the Fleet was away in one of its innumerable sweeps in search of the enemy.

To those Orcadians who earned their keep by fishing, the blocking of the eastern channels had virtually cut off their livelihood. To reach the rich fishing grounds off Eastern Orkney, the fishermen from Burray and South Ronaldsay now had to sail south through Scapa Flow to the treacherous waters of the Pentland Firth. This added time and more danger to an already-hazardous occupation.

Soon after the cessation of hostilities, Orkney County Council made representations to the Admiralty for removal of the blockships, but no action was taken until after March, 1920, when three islanders were lost in Skerry Sound. As a result, the *Aorangi* in Kirk Sound was removed by the end of September. This rendered Kirk Sound navigable but still dangerous. After two more years, political pressure induced the Admiralty to remove the hulk of the *Numidian* to widen Kirk Sound still further. The ship, however, was too badly holed to be re-floated, so she was swung around to lie to the east of the original line of blockships, parallel to the shore of mainland Orkney. The channel thus opened in Kirk Sound between *Numidian* and *Thames* to the south, was over 200 yards wide and about 40 feet deep at high tide.

This, however, was little help to the Burray fishermen, whose fleet was declining fast. After concerted political pressure, the hulk of *Lorne* in Water Sound was dispersed in 1931. (Attempts were made to raise *Thames* in Kirk Sound, but these were abandoned and the hull of the blockship later broke in two and settled deeper into the sand.) The remaining ships were a feature of the eastern coastline of the Flow for over a decade.

As war threatened in 1938 and 1939, the defences of the Fleet Anchorage again came under scrutiny. Early in 1939, two more blockships were sunk across the eastern channels, and Water Sound was again closed by a single blockship, SS *Majda*. The *Soriano* was now sunk in Kirk Sound between the decrepit *Thames* and the *Numidian*, and the channel between the sterns of *Soriano* and *Thames* was about 45 yards wide, partly blocked by heavy wire hawsers laid from each ship out across the gap and secured to anchors on the seabed. The north channel between the bow of *Soriano* and *Numidian* was 70 yards wide, but angled north-east across Kirk Sound. Another heavy hawser was stretched out due north from the bow of *Soriano* to an anchor close to the mainland shore. This, then, was exactly the situation when war broke out again in 1939.

Chapter 11
THE FINAL IRONY

A SERIES OF AGREEMENTS had been reached between the world's naval powers after the Great War, restricting the number and sizes of ships each country was permitted to build and maintain. As the years passed, Germany broke these agreements by building larger ships than she was permitted, and Japan refused even to be bound by treaties inhibiting her warship building plans. Britain, however, had kept within the treaties and commissioned only two battleships since the Great War. Thus, when war broke out again, Britain's capital ships were all elderly, and even though those remaining had become better equipped and protected as a result of refits, most of them dated from the Great War. One of these was HMS *Royal Oak*.

Laid down at Devonport Dockyard in January 1914, *Royal Oak* was completed and commissioned in May, 1916, and joined the Grand Fleet as a unit of Jellicoe's 4th Battle Squadron. She was a battleship of *Royal Sovereign*-class, (developments of the fast *Queen Elizabeth* class). They were designed to operate at 22 knots, as units of the Battle Fleet, and were fitted with the hard-hitting 15-inch guns which had proved to be very efficient. They differed in appearance from the *Queen Elizabeth's* in that their secondary 6-inch casemate guns were fitted further aft to afford them better protection from heavy seas. The 8-15 inch guns were mounted in twin turrets along the ship's centreline; 'B' and 'X' turrets were mounted one deck above 'A' and 'Y' turrets, thus superfiring. *Royal Oak* fired shells weighing 1,920lbs a distance of 24,400 yards, so could deliver a broadside weighing 6·85 tons almost 12½ miles, (against *König's* 4 tons and 10 miles at Jutland).

Her hull was divided and sub-divided into numerous

▲
HMS
Royal Oak
viewed
from stern
1937
(Imperial
War
Museum)

watertight compartments and her armoured deck was one deck higher than in predecessing British Dreadnoughts. This provided a greater reserve buoyancy and below-waterline integrity than any previous British warship. In the safety of harbour, however, many of the watertight doors and hatches would be open for maintenance parties and the crew going about their daily routines. In such situations, doors were open on opposite sides of the ship, (so a sailor crossed from port to starboard and back to pass through successive watertight bulkheads,) to protect against flooding if the ship was holed in port.

Steam for *Royal Oak* was generated by 18 large tube Yarrow three-drum boilers arranged in three boiler rooms midships. She was driven by two sets of Parsons marine turbines driving four shafts. On trials she developed 40,306 s.h.p. which would have driven her close to 22 knots.

At the Battle of Jutland she was not considered to be fully operational having only joined the Grand Fleet two weeks before. Nevertheless, at the end of the fighting she had contributed to the demise of *Wiesbaden,* damaged the boiler uptakes of *Derfflinger* and added to the already mounting problems on board *Seydlitz*. This was an impressive performance from a newly-commissioned ship. The remainder of her war was spent in Scapa Flow, or engaged in the repeated sweeps by the Grand Fleet across the North Sea, or in dock for maintenance work.

When the Fleets met to take the German ships to internment in November 1918, *Royal Oak,* (now a unit of the First Battle Squadron,) was fourth ship in the line formed off the German port side. After the scuttling, she received on board many of the German officers and men. The Germans complained later about their treatment on *Royal Oak*, alleging that their personal kit was looted and von Reuter's Admiral's coat was stolen. As far as is known, no disciplinary action was taken against the crew.

Royal Oak was allocated to the Atlantic Fleet after the dispersal of the Grand Fleet, and remained there until 1922, when she was taken into dock at Portsmouth for her first major refit. Longitudinal bulges were fitted on the sides of the hull covering the armour belt and extending down to the bilges. Their purpose was to improve the ship's protection against torpedo attack, and to correct the stability of the ship — as while she performed well in heavy seas, she heeled alarmingly when turning. The bulges added 14 feet to the beam of the ship and were constructed of 9/16-inch thick steel plate, subdivided internally both horizontally and vertically into watertight compartments. The addition of these bulges made the vessel able to withstand the detonation of a 750 lb torpedo warhead, and increased her stability without appreciable loss of speed. Further improvement to the ship's protection was to provide inboard compartments between the 15-inch magazines and the hull sides. They could be flooded with water to help absorb some of the shock of a torpedo explosion.

The ship's armament was increased by the replacement of the single 3-inch angle mountings with 4-inch high angle guns, and the addition of 4 three-pounder saluting guns. The rangefinders in 'B' and 'X' turrets were replaced with more accurate 30 ft instruments. Fire control systems for main and secondary armaments were modernised, and a high angle control station and rangefinder was mounted above the spotting top. *Royal Oak* left Portsmouth Dockyard in 1924, and in 1926 joined the Mediterranenan Fleet based at Malta, one of the most popular overseas postings. (Here, she became the top ship in the Fleet inter-ship competitions, individuals and teams successful in boxing, rowing and hockey.) In the late spring of 1927 she arrived at Devonport to receive a new spotting top. Two more 4-inch H.A. guns were fitted and two 6-inch guns were removed from her superstructure deck. She then returned to Malta as Flagship of the Second Division of the First Battle Squadron.

A clash of personalities now developed between *Royal Oak's* two senior officers and the Division's Rear Admiral, all newly appointed to her. The result was Courts Martial of the two officers, following which one left the service. The Rear Admiral was placed on the retired list. But with the appointment of replacement Captain and Commander, *Royal Oak* went from strength to strength to become the crack gunnery ship of the Mediterranean Fleet.

In 1934 she was taken into dock again for another major refit. Additional armour plate, up to 4 inches thick, was laid over her main deck to protect magazines and machinery, (but the weight reduced the vessel's reserve buoyancy and stability). The four single H.A. guns on the superstructure deck were replaced with four twin 4-inch high angle/low angle mountings, controlled from a new Mk III high angle control station (HACS) mounted on the spotting top. Sponsons were built each side of the base of the funnel on which were mounted 8 barrel 2-pounder pom-poms, and smaller sponsons erected each side of the conning tower forward supported two 0·5-inch quadruple machine gun mountings. The 6-inch gun director towers were moved to a new platform high up the foremast, and the mainmast was re-constructed as a heavy tripod mast to support a radio direction finder office and a second HACS. A slider catapult, type SIIT, for launching the ship's amphibious spotter-fighter aircraft, was mounted on 'X' turret, and an aircraft recovery crane was fitted on the port side of the superstructure deck. When *Royal Oak* re-commissioned in 1937, she was the best equipped of the *Royal Sovereign* class and joined the Home Fleet to be based at Scapa Flow.

After the outbreak of war, German reconnaissance aircraft took photographs over Scapa Flow of British ships at anchor and the state of the harbour's defences. These were passed to Commodore Karl Dönitz, (at that time Commodore of the Unterseeboote arm of the Kriegsmarine, but who was ultimately to become Deputy Führer, and for a brief time, Führer). He was convinced that his U-boats held the key to defeating Britain and was out to demonstrate this early in the war by sending a U-boat to force the British Fleet base and sink some of her still mighty capital ships. After studying the photographs and reports, Dönitz decided that such a mission could be successful given the right man. The opportunity was given to Lieutenant Günther Prien, Commander of the type VIIB U-boat, *U-47*. Following the necessary preparations, (which included replacing the compressed air-driven torpedoes with the electrically driven type G7e,) *U-47* sailed from her base at Kiel on Sunday, 8th October, 1939 — destination Scapa Flow!

On the day that *U-47* set off, *Royal Oak*, with two screening destroyers, was patrolling the Channel between Fair Isle and Orkney. Her mission was to prevent the German battlecruiser *Gneisenau* from breaking into the Atlantic where the Merchant convoys supplying Britain ran. *Gneisenau* had been reported off Norway and the British battlecruisers, *Hood* and *Repulse*, together with the newest battleships, *Nelson* and *Rodney*, and the aircraft carrier, *Furious,* with scouting cruisers and screening destroyers had set off across the North Sea to intercept her, leaving *Royal Oak* to close the gap between Orkney and Shetland. Gales blew their worst during the next day or so, and even a ship the size of *Royal Oak* suffered in the violent seas. Waves swept along her forecastle deck, damaging fittings and carrying away carley rafts, and water severely flooded the battery deck. Because of the conditions, not only did the British ships fail to locate *Gneisenau*, (which had escaped back to the Baltic,) but the German bombers sent to destroy the British ships, (for which *Gneisenau* was only the bait,) did not find them. The British were ordered back to port, and *Royal Oak* arrived back in Scapa Flow on October 11th.

To protect the capital ships from Luftwaffe attacks, all except *Royal Oak* were sent away from Scapa Flow. She lay in the north-east of the anchorage where her anti-aircraft guns could protect the important radio direction finding station at Netherbutton, near Kirkwall. Friday, 13th October, on *Royal Oak* was spent in clearing up the shambles below decks after her rough passage earlier in the week, and taking on board stores.

All that day *U-47* was lying on the bottom of the North Sea, 90 metres down, some miles to the east of Orkney. Prien had decided that *U-47* was to attempt to pass through Kirk Sound between *Soriano* and *Numidian* 30 minutes before high water, when the tide would be turning and the tidal race still. On the night of October 13th, spring tides ensured the maximum possible depth of water in Kirk Sound, and slack water occurred at almost 23.00. At 22.30, *U-47* surfaced and stealthily approached the narrows between Lamb Holm and mainland Orkney.

At 22.50, a merchant ship was spotted from the U-boat, forcing her to submerge until it had passed, and at 23.15, *U-47* re-surfaced and proceeded into Holm Sound, (the wide entrance to Kirk and Skerry Sounds). Prien had now missed slack water, and as depth soundings were noted, the navigation officer suddenly realised that they were heading into Skerry Sound — which the blockships made impenetrable! The U-boat swung hard to starboard and her engines pushed to the limit as she turned north. She grounded briefly, then freed herself and turned to port as Lamb Holm was passed on her port side. She was soon in Kirk Sound and switched to electric motors, (her diesels being too noisy,) and now being carried by the strongly running tide, *U-47* shot through the gap between the two northerly blockships, yawing from side to side like a wild thing. She caught on the hawser laid out from the bow of *Soriano*, but the combined energies of tide and engine forced her head round off the sand and she was swept into St Mary's Bay and headed into Scapa Flow. As she passed the village of St Mary's, however, (less than half a mile off her starboard beam,) car lights suddenly swept across the water towards them. The car stopped and those on the bridge of the U-boat must have felt completely exposed. Then the car turned and drove off towards Kirkwall and *U-47* pressed on into Scapa Flow to complete the job in hand — there was no turning back now.

The reconnaissance photographs had shown most of the capital ships lying at the World War I anchorages north of Flotta, which was where *U-47* now headed. She changed back to diesel engines, and soon Hoxa Sound and the boom defence drifters could be seen from the bridge. (Almost every witness describes the visibility conditions differently that night — from bright illumination to black, overcast and rain showers. All agree that an NNE wind force 3-4 was blowing.) As *U-47* approached the Main Fleet anchorage, Prien realised that there were no ships there! Not wishing to expose the U-boat to the drifters longer than necessary, at 00.12 he turned back to search north towards Scapa Bay, where the photographs had shown one or two heavy ships at anchor. There lay *Royal Oak* before him, bows to the north of east along both the direction of wind and the eddy current set up in Scapa Bay by the ebbing tide.

At about 01.00 and as the U-boat swung to starboard 3,000 metres away from the battleship, three torpedoes were fired from her forward tubes, another jamming. She turned tail and fired one more from her stern tube. Nearly four minutes later a single hit was heard, but *Royal Oak* remained dark and still. Turning back, *U-47* headed towards the stubborn battleship, and closing the range fired three more torpedoes. A little over three minutes later, three explosions were heard followed by brief, ominous tongues of yellow flame shooting upwards from around the ship's superstructure. *U-47* now beat a hasty retreat to force her way back out of the anchorage through the deeper, but narrower space in Kirk Sound between the wrecks of *Thames* and *Minieh*. Her engines were flat out and straining against the tidal flow pouring through at 10 knots.

Of the first four torpedoes fired, one struck *Royal Oak* a glancing blow on her starboard side, most of the blast deflecting outwards from the ship's side. Inboard *Royal Oak* at this point is the ship's inflammable stores, which were flooding rapidly. Fumes rising from below decks suggested that an internal explosion had occurred in the store, and a man was sent down the foredeck hatch ladder to investigate. Most of the crew were woken by the shock of the explosion, but many went back to sleep when told what was thought to be the cause. Then, the first and second torpedoes of *U-47's* second salvo, struck the ship within seconds of each other on her starboard bulge aft of midships. These sunk the ship. The lower bulge plating was torn apart, hull plating disintegrated and hull frames blasted aside; fuel oil tanks were ruptured and the longitudinal torpedo bulkhead within the ship was breached. A hole 30 feet in diameter appeared in the hull and water poured into her after boiler room and starboard wing turbine room. The last torpedo struck low down just aft of her bow, where the hull was narrow and unprotected, and blew the double bottom and lower platform deck clean out of the ship for about 30 feet. Many watertight doors were open, and water cascaded through, soon reaching generator rooms. All power was thus lost and *Royal Oak* was doomed. As she continued to list, her starboard middle deck scuttles became submerged, and water gushed in quickly adding to her lean. Soon her upper deck portholes were below water, and she capsized. By 01.30 all that was to be seen of *Royal Oak* was fuel oil and men desperately fighting for their lives. A total of 833 men died with her.

As though her loss had not been disaster enough, for it to have happened in the Home Fleet anchorage was a double blow to the Admiralty. (The Nazi propaganda machine capitalised to the full on Prien's remarkable feat of arms, albeit assisted by Britain's lack of readiness for war.) The immediate effect was to place three further blockships in Kirk Sound. (As it was not then known how *U-47* had got in, this action demonstrated that the precise weaknesses in the defences had been recognised even before the *Royal Oak* tragedy.)

THE FINAL IRONY

The ultimate security of the Eastern Channels began in May, 1940, when work began on the Churchill barriers to finally link South Ronaldsay and Burray to the mainland. About 1300 men were permanently at work on the scheme, including some 900 Italian prisoners of war. The barriers were sufficiently high in 1942 to prevent any repetition of the *Royal Oak* incident, and they were completed in 1944. The remains of some of the Second World War blockships can still be seen when driving across the barriers, and much more of each lies beneath the surface.

Royal Oak lies in 32 metres of water with her port bilge keel uppermost. Her decks are at an angle of about 40 degrees to the seabed and her masts lie out from beneath the hull, sheared off as her huge bulk turned over. The weight of her 15-inch gun barrels caused her turrets to slew round to starboard as she capsized, so their barrels are now buried deep into the bottom of Scapa Flow. Acting as levers under her massive weight, some have broken out of their trunnions and forced the turret top plates off, which now lie flat on the seabed.

Close to the site of *Royal Oak* now floats a conventional green conical channel buoy on which a plaque advises: 'This marks the wreck of HMS *Royal Oak* and the grave of her crew. Respect their resting place. Unauthorised diving prohibited.'

Royal Navy divers visit the wreck annually to carry out a survey, and replace the white ensign, hoisting it under water each year. A moving memorial service and wreath-laying ceremony is then conducted over the site. Every year, on the Saturday falling closest to the anniversary of her sinking, the remaining survivors gather together at the Naval War Memorial on Southsea Common at Portsmouth, her home base, to hold a service in memory of their lost shipmates. The Royal Navy, survivors, relatives and Orcadians all remember and respect: so must we all.

Appendix 1
SHIPS INTERNED AND THEIR FATE

BATTLECRUISERS

von der Tann	Raised by Cox and Danks	1930
Moltke	Raised by Cox and Danks	1927
Seydlitz	Raised by Cox and Danks	1928
Hindenburg	Raised by Cox and Danks	1930
Derfflinger	Raised by Metal Industries	1939

BATTLESHIPS

Kaiserin	Raised by Metal Industries	1936
Kaiser	Raised by Cox and Danks	1929
Friedrich der Grosse	Raised by Metal Industries	1937
Prinzregent Luitpold	Raised by Cox and Danks	1931
König Albert	Raised by Metal Industries	1935
König	At Scapa Flow	
Grosser Kurfürst	Raised by Metal Industries	1938
Markgraf	At Scapa Flow	
Kronprinz Wilhelm	At Scapa Flow	
Bayern	Raised by Metal Industries	1934
Baden	Beached: used in R.N. gunnery tests finally sunk in 1921 off Portsmouth	

LIGHT CRUISERS

Brummer	At Scapa Flow	
Bremse	Raised by Cox and Danks	1929
Emden	Not sunk: handed over to France	
Dresden	At Scapa Flow	
Frankfurt	Beached: refloated by R.N.; handed over to U.S.A.	
Karlsruhe	At Scapa Flow	
Köln	At Scapa Flow	
Nürnberg	Beached: retained by Britain; Used in Gunnery Tests and finally sunk in 1922 off Portsmouth	

DESTROYERS

S32	Raised by Cox and Danks	1925
S36	Raised by Cox and Danks	1925
G38	Raised by Cox and Danks	1928
G39	Raised by Cox and Danks	1927
G40	Raised by Cox and Danks	1926
V43	Beached by R.N.; to U.S.A.	
V44	Raised by Cox and Danks	1925
V45	Raised by Scapa Flow Salvage	1924
V46	Beached by R.N.; to France	
S49	Beached by R.N.; retained by Britain	
S50	Beached by R.N.; retained by Britain	

S51	Beached by R.N.; retained by Britain	
S52	Raised by Cox and Danks	1924
S53	Raised by Cox and Danks, subsequently foundered	1927
S54	Raised by Cox and Danks, subsequently foundered	1924
S55	Raised by Cox and Danks	1925
S56	Raised by Cox and Danks	1926
S60	Beached by R.N.; to Japan	
S65	Raised by Cox and Danks	1926
V70	Raised by Cox and Danks	1929
V73	Beached by R.N.; retained by Britain	
V78	Raised by Cox and Danks	1925
V80	Beached by R.N.; to Japan	
V81	Beached by R.N.; foundered on way to breakers	
V82	Beached by R.N.; retained by Britain	
V83	At Scapa Flow	
G86	Raised by Cox and Danks	1926
G89	Raised by Cox and Danks	1926
G91	Raised by Cox and Danks	1925
G92	Beached by R.N.; retained by Britain	
V100	Beached by R.N.; to France	
G101	Raised by Cox and Danks	1926
G102	Beached by R.N.; to U.S.A.	
G103	Raised by Cox and Danks, subsequently foundered	1925
G104	Raised by Cox and Danks	1926
B109	Raised by Cox and Danks	1926
B110	Raised by Cox and Danks	1926
B111	Raised by Cox and Danks	1926
B112	Raised by Cox and Danks	1926
V125	Beached by R.N.; retained by Britain	
V126	Beached by R.N.; to France	
V127	Beached by R.N.; to Holland	
V128	Beached by R.N.; retained by Britain	
V129	Raised by Cox and Danks	1925
S131	Raised by Scapa Flow Salvage	1924
S132	Beached by R.N.; to U.S.A.	
S136	Raised by Cox and Danks	1928
S137	Beached by R.N.; retained by Britain	
S138	Raised by Cox and Danks	1926
H145	Raised by Cox and Danks	1928

Appendix 2
UNDERWATER LIFE ON THE WRECKS

THIS BOOK could not be complete without some reference to the abundance of marine life on the German wrecks. Those who enjoy every aspect of the forays beneath the waves, will appreciate the sight of the perfectly orientated pollack passing by as much as the brass pedestal of the rudder indicator before them.

Arriving on the upper surfaces of the wrecks, the diver is immediately struck by the absence of life around him. On closer examination, however, (particularly in torchlight when colours are enhanced,) there are specimens of the tiny Devonshire Cup Coral (Caryophyllia smithii) and the white-tentacled, orange-centred anemone, *Actinothoe sphyrodeta*. The fore-part of *Dresden* is particular densely populated with these species, and solitary examples of another species of anemone, the Plumose Anemone *(Metridium senile)* are found on most wrecks. Common Brittle Starfish *(Ophiothrix fragilis)* populate the upper surfaces, together with examples of the Feather Star *(Antedon bifida)*. The Common Sea Urchin *(Echinus esculentus)* is in abundance on all the wrecks, and all the overhangs on the hulls, superstructures and fittings support the soft coral known as Dead Men's Fingers *(Alcyonium digitatum)*, as shown in the photographs of the parts of the wrecks in this book.

Sponge growths are particularly difficult to identify without studying samples under a microscope. Of the flat, encrusting sponges, the grey coloured, leathery textured *Pachymatisma johnstonia,* and the red, tough textured *Mycale rotalis,* both form sheets of irregularly shaped growth covering areas up to perhaps half a square metre, and are found on the shallower wrecks, notably *Karlsruhe* and *V83,* as well as on *Bremse.* One species of rare sponge (found only around Orkney and Shetland in British waters,) exists between overhangs and inside openings within the ships' hulls. This sponge, *Sycandra utriculus,* hangs vertically beneath horizontal surfaces, and can take various forms, from long pendulous shapes of up to one metre long, to shorter, lobed forms. The sponge is beige, which blends well against rust and sediment. In some forms this sponge is very similar to the far more common Purse Sponge *(Grantia compressa)* but is generally larger.

A number of varieties of the Sea Squirt family are found on all the wrecks. *Ascidiella aspersia,* a longish, grey specimen with its fluted syphon at the extreme top and the atrial syphon lower down, is one of the most common, together with *Ciona intestinalis,* which is longer and has the top syphon edge scalloped rather than fluted. There is also the Light Bulb Tunicate *(Clavelina lepadiformis)*, a transparent mass measuring 5-10cm across, and comprising tiny, tubular organisms. These animals 'inhale' water through the top syphon which is then filtered through crude gills within the body, where minute particles are digested in a rudimentary digestive system. The filtered water is then exhaled through the lower syphon.

The wrecks are relatively rich in species of molluscs. A number of varieties of Sea Slugs inhabit their outer surfaces, which take time and patience to observe. These include *Colpodaspis pusilla*, a white, snail-like specimen about 5mm long with an internal shell; *Dendronotus frondosus*, a pink or mottled brown animal with branching gills and feather-like appendages along its back; and *Doto fragilis*, with a pale brown body and again with gills and appendages along its body. The largest of these uniquely attractive creatures measures only 1cm.

Much more easily identifiable are the many bi-valve shells found on the seabed around the wrecks. These include Horse Mussels *(Modiolus modiolus)*, the Great Scallop *(Pecten maximus)*, which have provided lunch on dive boats; Queen Scallops *(Aequipecten opercularis)*, another tasty dish—but being smaller, they take longer to collect in sufficient quantities! They are easily recognised as they swim along by opening and closing their shells, (jokingly likened to a pair of false teeth swimming through the water!)

Within the wrecks, there is generally an absence of large forms of marine life, the most commonly seen species being small Spider Crabs *(Macropodia tenuirostris* or *Macropodia rostrata)* and an occasional rust-stained Edible Crab *(Cancer pagurus)*, sometimes found buried in the sediment on the wrecks. Fish are notably absent from the deeper wrecks, with the exception of Butterfish *(Pholis gunnellus)*, which is found hiding in the crevices, and Goldsinny *(Centrolabrus rupestris)* which are commonly seen feeding in the sediment disturbed by the passing diver's fins. The shallower wrecks support Ballan Wrasse *(Labrus bergylta)* in their various colour forms, from pale gold mottled with light brown to blue-green with distinctive orange highlights, picked out by the sun's rays filtering through the clear water.

The decompressing diver need not be bored during his 'stops', as the water has planktonic animals too numerous to list, let alone identify. Easily visible are the transparent medusae of the Hydroid, *Rathkea octopunctata* and *Bougainvillia ramosa*, which are a phase in the lifecycle of these bottom-dwelling animals. These medusae are bell or umbrella shaped with their internal organs visible through the transparent walls, and small tentacles surround the edge of the dome. Numerous other tiny animals abound: oval-shaped discs fringed with diminutive

beating cilia are perhaps the Planula stage of the lifecycle of the

Common Jellyfish *(Aurelia aurita),* of which there are many adult specimens in the Flow. Occasionally seen, is the blue-ish jellyfish, *Cyanea lamarckii.* From the periphery of its umbrella trail long tentacles, inside which are large, frilly mouth arms. (This jellyfish will sting exposed faces and arms.)

This is by no means a complete list of marine life in Scapa Flow, but is intended to assist identification of some of the species, and demonstrate that there is more to diving the German ships than the man-made structures themselves. Perhaps these wrecks require a detailed study by marine biologists who may discover some species which has evolved to suit these circumstances.

Appendix 3
LYNESS

AS THE FORMER NAVAL BASE and centre of operations for the salvaging of the German Fleet, Lyness has become a natural haunt for visiting divers, and because of the history surrounding the port, is well worth a visit. Although not an important part of the First World War, Lyness had begun to be developed as the Naval base for the Fleet towards the end of the conflict. Work commenced on building a dock wall and establishing shore facilities during 1917, but the base did not become fully operational until 1919. It became redundant soon after as the British Fleet was dispersed about the Empire. The original stone wharf was constructed by Kinnear and Moodie of Glasgow, who introduced the first ever steam locomotives into Orkney, which transported the stone quarried from behind the wharf to the new workings. During 1919, the base became HQ for the Commanding Officer, North of Scotland, until late 1920, when Lyness was no longer a Naval Base.

During 1924, Cox and Danks established their salvage operations headquarters at the now disused site, utilising the remaining buildings as workshops, accommodation for their workforce which numbered up to 200, and even a cinema. The hull of the light cruiser, *Bremse,* and a number of destroyers were dismantled at Lyness, and offshore some of the super-structure was removed from the inverted big ships, (where it still litters the seabed,) to facilitate their towing to the Forth. Bridge structures, masts, cranes and guns litter the bottom from Lyness northwards through Gutter Sound. Cox and Danks' successors, Metal Industries, also used Lyness and improved the facilities of their workforce, (the majority of whom were former Cox and Danks employees).

During the late 1930s, as war again threatened, work began to secretly instal a labyrinth of communications and pipe tunnels and fortified underground fuel storage tanks, in preparation for the re-establishment of Lyness as a major Naval Base. During 1939, a boom defence HQ was set up, and four 4.5 inch anti-aircraft guns were emplaced around 12 newly-built surface oil tanks, together with machine guns landed from the warships which began again to regularly visit Scapa Flow. With the outbreak of war, Lyness became the base for the Home Fleet, which was to blockade Germany by denying access to her ships through the North Sea to the Atlantic.

On August 26th, 1939, HMS *Iron Duke,* the now partly demilitarised Flagship of the British Grand Fleet at Jutland,

arrived off Lyness to act as HQ for the Admiral Commanding

Orkney and Shetland (ACOS), and as the mail sorting depot and stores ship. Seven weeks later, she was holed by bombs from attacking German Junkers 88 bombers, and beached in Longhope Bay where she remained for the duration of the war, serving amongs other things as 'jankers' ship. Lyness now became HQ for ACOS and his staff, who finally moved into the purpose built, austere-looking building still standing at Wee Fea beyond the Naval Cemetery.

The quay alongside which the dive charter boats now lie was completed in 1944. (Because of its high cost, it became known as 'Golden Wharf'.) The three piers still to be seen in Ore Bay, south of Lyness, were all built during the last war. The two steel piers, (one the most northerly and the other across the bay to the south at Rinnigal), were in use in 1941, while the concrete pier between them to the west took a year longer to complete. The North pier was used for Naval ferries, water boats and provision ships; the West pier was for tugs and small craft, while the South pier was used for landing stores and hydrogen cyclinders for barrage balloons.

The run-down of Lyness as a Naval Base began in 1944. The British Home Fleet had been dispersed and the barrage balloons were taken south to help defend the industrial cities of England. After the end of World War II, three German escort vessels, and a destroyer were brought as part of the War reparations, and were anchored off Lyness.

Lyness continued to be used as a re-fuelling depot for HM ships, which still called at Scapa Flow, and employed up to 150 maintaining services for the warships. The depot was used less and less, however, and finally closed down in March 1957. Most of the buildings and fuel tanks were subsequently demolished, or fell down, and the underground pipe ducts and trunkings became overgrown and the haunt of rabbits. In 1977, the Orkney Islands Council bought the former base from the Ministry of Defence, and work is now underway to establish it as a museum. While the modern visitor to Orkney appreciates the rugged, spectacular scenery, prolific bird life, clear waters and historical sites on the islands, typical memories of those who were posted there during the war are personified by a friend from North Wales, who spent the first two years of his war at Lyness:

> 'One is supposed only to remember the good times, but I'm afraid my memories of Orkney consist of gales with horizontal rain, almost continuous darkness, mud, bitter cold, miserable living quarters, and on top of all that, shrapnel from our own shells falling all around us during air raids, which we thought more dangerous than Jerry's bombs!'

He would probably hardly recognise Lyness today! Although the Post Office is housed in a former M-o-D building, and one oil tank still stands, gone are most of the huts and sheds which formed the base. The Second World War pumphouse now forms the centrepiece of the Orkney Islands Council Scapa Flow Interpretation Project. Photographic displays detailing the history of Scapa Flow and the Lyness naval base are arranged among the restored pump machinery. The pumps and driving engines gleam with fresh paint and polished brasswork, and next door to them, the boilers look as though they could fire up at any time. The first phase of this well-conceived project is nearly complete, with the establishment of a mock NAAFI cafe, but there are plans to rehabilitate the remaining oil storage tank for an audiovisual presentation, reinstate some of the naval base railway track to run an authentic diesel locomotive, and add to the growing collection of artefacts. These include a 5.9-inch gun from one of the scuttled German Fleet Warships, a pair of machine guns and a Rolls Royce 'Merlin' engine (salvaged from a Spitfire which crashed in Scapa Flow during the last war), one of the steam cranes which serviced the base during that conflict and the great bronze propeller from HMS *Hampshire*. The collection continues to grow, and Lyness pumphouse will provide a unique insight for future generations into the maritime and naval history of wartime Orkney.

A short walk past the oil tank is the Naval Cemetery, dedicated in June, 1915, where simple stones mark the resting places of many sailors. Hundreds were washed ashore after HMS *Hampshire,* with Lord Kitchener aboard, struck a mine on the 5th June, 1916. Almost 700 died, including Lord Kitchener, when the ship went down. Later stones mark the resting places of some who died following the sinking of HMS *Royal Oak* in 1939. Unlike the *Hampshire* incident, most who died in this attack went down with the ship.

The Cemetery is immaculate, and it can be seen from the visitors' book that many who call at Lyness feel it necessary to pay their respects to those who died to protect our way of life. Perhaps but for their sacrifice, our visits to their resting place could not be possible.

Appendix 4
A DIVER'S TALES

DURING RESEARCHES for this book, I was fortunate enough to chat with one Sandy Robertson, a remarkably lucid 80-year-old ex-diver with both Cox and Danks and Metal Industries, (and subsequently world-wide,) who is now living in well-earned retirement on Hoy. By the fire in his cosy lounge one afternoon, Sandy reminisced on his experiences working in Scapa Flow.

Sandy explained to me how difficult it had been, and what great physical effort was demanded, to drill and thread the steel hull plating of the German ships, to screw in the bolts to which were attached the airlock stay wires. The heavy wire stays then had to be dragged along the hull bottom to the appropriate fixing eye, pulled through, and secured with rope clamps. The hull plating had now to be drilled and the holes threaded to accept studs fitted with large washers and nuts, which would be used to temporarily clamp down the bottom flange of the airlock. To work accurately 30 metres down, looking through the tiny faceplate of the helmet, would have been no easy task, even using a template.

The struggles the diver encountered in locating and securing the airlocks, (some of which were over 100 feet high and weighed up to 20 tons), suspended as they were from crane jibs pivoted from floating barges, defeated even Sandy's rhetoric. Once the flanges were clamped to the hull, the ends of the stay wires had to be passed up to the top of the airlocks to be secured and tensioned. Many of the stays were attached to the airlocks below water level, so much of this work was done by the diver. While visibility underwater in Scapa Flow is remarkably good, the lie of a stay wire could still not be seen along its entire length. Sandy well remembers the dressing down received if, on the ship's surfacing, the occasional wire was crossed with that of another airlock!

The diver's work in attaching the airlocks was not yet finished, as the hull had now to be drilled and tapped for the final bolting down of the airlock bottom flange. It had been pre-drilled on the surface so at least these bolt holes provided the diver with an accurate template for this task. The airlocks were bolted down with 50 one-inch diameter bolts.

Apart from fitting airlocks, the diver's work involved initially surveying the wrecks, reporting on the lie, angle of heel and condition. He also sealed hull openings to make the ship airtight for lifting. Such work was difficult enough if the diver was on a flat surface, but even worse if the opening was halfway up the vertical side of the hull, where the diver would be working in mid-water.

I enquired how the divers had coped with decompression? 'No problem' was Sandy's reply, 'we simply hung in the water on our safety lines at the end of each shift.'

I then remarked that I had not realised that they had worked in shifts. 'Aye', he said, 'two each day, so with time taken for dressing and undressing we would spend 2½-3 hours underwater each shift.'

'So it must have been a long day with a six-hour interval between dives,' I observed.

'Why no, just an hour and a half was spent on the surface between dives,' he replied. I pointed out that if they had been working on the seabed at up to 18 fathoms (not for Sandy any fancy metric measurements!) they must have endured uncomfortably long decompression stops at the end of their second dive.

'Always the same,' said Sandy, 'five minutes at 20 feet and fifteen minutes at 10 feet at the end of every shift'! He qualified this by explaining that any work carried out at depth was completed first before moving up the hull to finish the shift in shallower water. Apparently, some of the older divers occasionally suffered bends and were decompressed in a surface chamber, but he could not remember any instances of his own age-group suffering decompression sickness: 'We were young and fit in those days. Unbreakable'—was his summary.

I commented that Ernest Cox must have been a great driving force behind his team to have achieved all he did at Scapa Flow. Sandy's expletives are unprintable! He explained that every Friday, 10% of the 200 workforce were sacked. Whether or not any of them were taken back the following Monday was dependent upon how many new applicants there were for work that morning. The simplest error, therefore, or the slightest sign of slackness during the week, could put you out of work from the next Friday. This was how Cox and Danks Ltd. produced such endeavour from their men; but, to be fair, many other employers in Britain used the same methods during the lean years of the 1920s and '30s.

Sandy had spent some time working inside the partly pumped out hulls of the upturned capital ships, and explained that while the stench of oil and rotting marine life was indescribable, they soon became accustomed to it. He also described the fun and games to be had in dodging the blue flames of methane gas ignited by their burning gear, as it spiralled and cartwheeled around in the confined spaces. It never occurred to them that a large pocket of gas could have blown them all up. That is until the arrival of the chemist, Cowan, who instigated and carried out regular tests within the hulls and had the working spaces flushed out with clean air at frequent

intervals. Cowan was very highly thought of by the men working inside the ships, as they appreciated that his efforts alone prevented many serious accidents.

Work on the partly-submerged light cruiser, *Bremse,* was hampered by the persistent ignition of her fuel oil which had spilled and spread throughout the ship. Some of the men soon saw the opportunity to have time off, as once the oil had ignited all hands would be evacuated. Cox, who was nobody's fool, finally set fire to all the oil, leaving the wreck to burn out. For days, a huge pall of black smoke hung over Swanbister Bay while the oil was consumed. Work on *Bremse* proceeded at record pace following this solution, as conditions inside the hull were revolting!

Some of Sandy's tales were tragic, such as those of his first dives on *Royal Oak* only the day after her sinking; others were hilarious, such as how the authorities mis-calculated slack water when they were attempting to place blockships in position in the fast-flowing currents between the eastern Orkney islands. All his tales were entertaining, and I shall be forever indebted to him for his insights, and for his reminiscences of the arduous life of the standard dress diver of 50-60 years ago.

Appendix 5
DIVING IN PRACTICE

DIVING WITHIN the confines of Scapa Flow is no more hazardous than diving the 'Tourist' routes of the Mediterranean sea; no currents threaten to sweep the diver away or jam him against small openings. The water is clear and diving operations are conducted from large, well-found vessels. What dangers there are lie not so much within the wrecks, but within the divers themselves.

With the exception of one cruiser, all the big German ships lie in deep water for SCUBA diving—more than 30 metres. Although the top of their mighty hulks are considerably shallower, few divers will wish to fin along flat, uninteresting hull plates, preferring instead to look at guns, bridges, cranes and conning towers. Thus, the visiting diver must be experienced in diving to such depths before coming to Orkney. This may take up to 50 or so dives, conducted over a year or two, before the diver is both competent and confident. Some may need many more dives to achieve this standard, and there are those who will never progress to such depths.

Irrespective of previous experience, the visiting diver should do a series of progressively deeper dives, culminating at the target depth in the wecks before coming to Orkney. Because of the vagaries of British weather, such dives may only be possible in inland fresh waters, with clear access to the surface. When wreck diving, added to the depth of water is the awesome spectacle of a huge ship rising above the diver, its shadow reducing light. Rigging wires, crane jibs and booms also restrict direct access to the surface. Only by wreck-diving elsewhere is it possible to gain experience of this, but if the diver can cope with the depth, the wrecks will be a spectacle of magnificence rather than objects of trepidation.

Ultimately, the adventurous diver will want to go inside the wrecks. Some compartments are dimly lit from light through portholes, while others are in inky blackness. Therefore, the diver should thoroughly familiarise himself with the exterior of the ship, which will take many dives. Only the foolhardy will pass inside a hatchway not knowing where on the ship he is. Another potential problem is the deep sediment formed by the remains of generations of marine life on the wrecks. This is stirred up by the diver's fins as he moves around, and forms clouds of silt reducing visibility to zero within seconds. Also, doors and hatchways were designed for fit and agile sailors, and are normally small. The SCUBA diver with a cylinder on his back and life jacket on his chest can only pass through with difficulty, and once through, finding his way back can become a nightmare. It is important to suppress feelings of panic in this situation, and the diver must also leave a line paid out behind him, its end secured outside the wreck to enable him to find his way out. This line is ideally a surface marker buoy reel line, with the buoy removed and a spring clip attached in its place. Without it, venturing inside the wrecks is suicidal!

Because of the depths involved, decompression diving may be envisaged. If so, then the technique of clipping the surface marker buoy reel line to the shotline dropped to mark the wreck could be considered. This way, the diver can ascend up the shotline to carry out the decompression stops in safety. Allowing the line to reel out as he fins along the wreck, the diver would reel back in as he finned back at the end of the dive. The use of floating surface marker buoys is not practicable as the line could easily snag or cut. It would be possible, however, to use a buoy which can be inflated on the bottom by the diver towards the end of his dive, and sent up to the surface on the surface marker buoy reel line as he holds off the ratchet pawl. When the reel stops running out, the buoy has reached the surface. The diver then winds in the reel as he ascends to his decompression stops. A word of warning, however, about this technique. The reel must be totally reliable, not stiff or likely to jam, as if it does, the diver will be dragged up too quickly by the ascending buoy, risking embolisms and decompression sickness. To avoid such an accident, the reel lanyard should be detached from the diver, and the reel held in the hand so that it can be immediately let go if necessary. This technique should be practised at progressively deeper depths in clear, still water until the diver becomes totally confident. Scapa Flow is not the place to practice any new techniques.

In the event of a diver becoming lost or trapped within a wreck, his partner could send up the inflatable marker buoy, and attach the reel lanyard at the opening on the wreck through which the lost diver entered. This would enable the searching diver to know where he was last seen, and so save precious time. On the tragic occasions when divers have been lost inside the wrecks in Scapa Flow, none had gone far inside. It may be that spare breathing sets taken down promptly to the right area could have made a difference to the outcome.

It is not the author's intention to argue the merits of one decompression table over another. I was taught to dive to RN Table 11, and have never seen the need to change from it.

In the preceding chapters, I have described a dive on each ship, to point out areas of interest to assist the newcomer to Scapa Flow in orientating himself on the wrecks. Space prohibits explicit details of how each dive was conducted, but the foregoing techniques, (which I am sure are not unique among experienced divers,) have all been used by the author on various dives. The reader will be able to use his imagination as to which technique is the most suitable for the dives described. Similarly, to save space, many dives on a wreck have been condensed into one described within the text. The safe diver, however, should never try to exceed his physical capabilities at these depths, as over-exertion leads to decompression complications as well as adding to the effects of nitrogen narcosis.

To enjoy diving in Scapa Flow to the full, it is important to see that all equipment is pristine, and for the diver to 'dive-up' beforehand to prepare for the depths involved. If the reader follows the accepted diving practices together with those I have outlined, he too will enjoy his holiday and will keep his diving safe.

Appendix 6
TECHNICAL DETAILS

KÖNIG-CLASS BATTLESHIPS

BUILDERS: *König:* Imperial Dockyard, Wilhelmshaven.
Completed August 1914.
Markgraf: Weser, Bremen.
Completed October 1914.
Kronprinz: Krupp Germaniawerft, Kiel.
Completed November 1914.

DIMENSIONS: Length overall: 177.7 metres. Length waterline
175.7 metres.
Beam (extreme): 30 metres. Beam (waterline)
29.5 metres.
Nominal draught: 8.3 metres. Deep load
draught: 9.29 metres.
Nominal displacement: 25,797 tonnes.
Deep load displacement: 29,669 tonnes.

ARMOUR: Krupp Cemented Nickel Alloy Steel.
Lower belt from aft: 130mm thick increasing to
350mm at after magazines; 350mm along hull to
forward magazines, reducing to 80mm thick at
bow.
Armoured deck: 120mm thick over rudder
machinery.
100mm over after torpedo rooms.
30mm thick beneath superstructure.
60mm from fore barbette to bow.
All decks within hull above
armoured deck 30mm thick
mild steel.
Main turrets: Front faces 300mm, sides 300mm
reducing to 250mm, roof 110mm
reducing to 80mm, back 150mm.
Barbettes: 300mm reducing to 200mm at junction
with armoured deck.
Casemates: 170mm.
Conning tower: 350mm front reducing to 170mm
rear.

ARMAMENT: 10-30.5cm/50 calibre guns in twin 'Drescheiben
Lafette C/11' turrets.
Max. elevation 13½° (16° from October 1916). *111*

Range 18,750 metres (20,480 metres from October 1916).

14-15cm/45 calibre on single enclosed pedestal mountings.

Max. elevation 20°.

Range 13,500 metres.

6-8.8cm/45 calibre on single enclosed pedestal mountings.

Max. elevation 30° (removed in October 1916).

2-8.8cm/45 calibre AA on single shielded pedestal mountings.

Max. elevation 60° (Increased to 4 guns in October 1916).

5-50cm torpedo tubes.

MACHINERY: 3 Parsons turbines direct to 3 shafts.
15 Schultz-Thorneycroft three drum superheated boilers. 12 coal-fired, 3 oil-fired. Working pressure 235psi.
Nominal rating: 31,000 shp.
Max. speed: 21 knots.

FUEL CAPACITY: 3,597 tonnes coal, 700 tonnes oil.

RANGE: 4,600 miles at 19 knots.

COMPLEMENT: *König* (as Squadron Flagship) 1,129.
Markgraf and *Kronprinz* 1,033.

BRUMMER LIGHT CRUISER

BUILDER: Vulcan, Stettin.

DIMENSIONS: Length overall: 140.35 metres. Length waterline 135 metres.
Beam: 13.2 metres.
Draught: 6.0 metres.
Nominal displacement: 4,385 tonnes. Deep load displacement: 5,856 tonnes.

ARMOUR: Hull sides: 40mm thick.
Armoured deck: 15mm thick.
Conning tower: 100mm front reducing to 20mm rear.
Gunshields: 50mm.

TECHNICAL DETAILS

ARMAMENT: 4-15cm/45 calibre shielded guns on pedestal
      mountings.
      Elevation angle 19°.
      2-8.8cm/45 calibre AA single guns on shielded
      pedestal mountings.
      Elevation angle 70°.
      2-50cm/torpedo launchers deck mounted.
      Capacity for 360 mines.

MACHINERY: 2-turbines direct drive to 2 shafts.
      6 three drum superheated boilers. 4 oil-fired,
      2 coal-fired.
      Nominal rating: 33,000 shp.
      Max. speed: 34 knots.

FUEL CAPACITY: 1,000 tonnes oil, 600 tonnes coal.

RANGE: 1,400 miles at 25 knots.

COMPLEMENT: 309.

KARLSRUHE LIGHT CRUISER

BUILDER: Imperial Dockyard, Wilhelmshaven.
      Completed December 1916.

DIMENSIONS: Length overall: 151.4 metres. Length waterline:
      145.8 metres.
      Beam: 14.3 metres.
      Draught: 6.32 metres.
      Displacement: 5,440 tonnes. Deep load
      displacement: 7,125.

ARMOUR: Belt: 18mm at ends increasing to 60mm over
      magazines and machinery spaces.
      Deck: 40mm, but 60mm over magazines.
      Conning tower: 100mm.
      Gunshields: 50mm.

ARMAMENT: 8-15cm/45 calibre guns on single shielded
      pedestal mountings.
      Elevation angle 22°.
      2-8.8cm/45 calibre AA on single shielded
      pedestal mountings.
      Elevation angle 80°.
      2-50cm torpedo launchers, deck mounted.
      Capacity for 120 mines.

TECHNICAL DETAILS

MACHINERY: 2-turbines single reduction geared to two shafts.
12 three drum superheated boilers. 10 coal,
2 oil-fired.
Nominal rating: 31,000 shp.
Max. speed: 29 knots.

FUEL CAPACITY: Coal 1,340 tonnes, oil 500 tonnes.

RANGE: 1,200 miles at 27 knots.

COMPLEMENT: 475.

KÖLN AND DRESDEN LIGHT CRUISERS

BUILDER: _Köln:_ Blohm & Voss, Hamburg.
Completed January 1918.
Dresden: Howaldtswerke, Kiel.
Completed March 1918.

DIMENSIONS: Length overall: 155.5 metres. Length waterline:
149.8 metres.
Beam: 14.3 metres.
Draught: 6.43 metres.
Displacement: 5,620 tonnes. Deep load
displacement: 7,486 tonnes.

ARMOUR: 18mm at ends increasing to 60mm over magazines
and machinery spaces.
Deck: 40mm increasing to 60mm over magazines.
Conning tower: 100mm.
Gunshields: 50mm.

ARMAMENT: 8-15cm/45 calibre guns on single shielded
pedestal mountings.
Elevation angle 22°.
2-8.8cm/45 calibre AA guns on single shielded
mountings.
Elevation angle 80°.
4-60cm torpedo launchers deck mounted.
Capacity for 120 mines.

MACHINERY: 2 turbines single reduction geared to two shafts.
14 three drum superheated boilers, 8 coal-fired
and 6 oil-fired.
Nominal rating: 49,000 shp.
Max. speed: 29 knots.

FUEL CAPACITY: Coal 1,100 tonnes, oil 1,050 tonnes.

RANGE: 1,200 miles at 27 knots.

COMPLEMENT: 559.

V83 DESTROYER

BUILDER: Vulcan, Hamburg. Completed July 1916.

DIMENSIONS: Length overall: 82 metres. Length waterline:
81 metres.
Beam: 8.3 metres.
Draught: 3.4 metres.
Displacement: 924 tonnes. Deep load
displacement: 1,188 tonnes.

ARMAMENT: 3-105mm/45 calibre guns on single open
mountings.
6-50cm torpedo launchers deck mounted.
Capacity for 24 mines.

MACHINERY: 2 turbines single reduction geared to two shafts.
3 three drum superheated boilers. Oil-Fired.
Nominal rating: 24,400 shp.
Max. speed: 36.5 knots.

FUEL CAPACITY: 306 tonnes.

RANGE: 1,810 miles at 20 knots.

COMPLEMENT: 87.

UB-116 U-BOAT

BUILDER: Blohm & Voss, Hamburg.
Completed November 1917.

DIMENSIONS: length: 55.9 metres.
Beam: 5.8 metres.
Draught: 3.8 metres.
Displacement: 519 tonnes (surface),
649 tonnes (submerged).

TECHNICAL DETAILS

ARMAMENT: 4-50 cm torpedo tubes (bow) 1-50cm torpedo tube (stern).
1-10.5cm/45 calibre gun.

MACHINERY: 2-6 cylinder diesel engines 1,100 bhp.
2-electric motors 788 bhp.
Max speed: 13.6 knots surface;
7.5 knots submerged.

FUEL CAPACITY: 86 tonnes oil.

MAX. DIVING DEPTH: 50 metres.

RANGE: 7,000 miles at 6 knots surface, 55 miles at 4 knots submerged.

HMS VANGUARD

CLASS: St Vincent (three ships)

BUILDER: Vickers, Barrow-in-Furness.
Completed February 1910.

DIMENSIONS: Length overall: 536ft.
Beam: 84ft.
Draught: 27ft 11in.
Displacement: 19,560 tons. Deep load
displacement 20.030 tons.

ARMOUR: Belt: 10in. tapering to 7in.
Aroured deck: 3in., other decks within hull: ¾in.
Turret faces: 11in.
Barbettes: 9in. tapering to 5in. at junction of
armoured deck.
Conning tower: 11in. front, reducing to 8in rear.

ARMAMENT: 10-12 inch/50 calibre MK XI guns in twin
turrets.
Max. elevation 15°.
Range: 21,200 yards.
20-4 inch/50 calibre QF on single pedestal
mountings.
3 submerged 18 inch torpedo tubes.

MACHINERY: Two sets Parsons turbines direct to 4 shafts. 18 Yarrow three drum large tube boilers with superheaters. Coal-fired with supplementary oil burners. Working pressure 250 p.s.i. Nominal rating: 24,500 shp. Max. speed: 21 knots.

FUEL CAPACITY: 2,800 tons coal, 940 tons oil, 190 tons patent fuel.

RANGE: 7,000 miles at 10 knots.

COMPLEMENT: 850.

HMS ROYAL OAK

CLASS: Royal Sovereign (five ships).

BUILDER: Devonport, Dockyard. Completed May 1916.

DIMENSIONS: Length overall: 620ft 6in.
Beam (as built): 88ft 6in. (after bulges fitted: 102ft 1in.)
Draught: Design load: 28ft 6in. Deep load 32ft 6in. (Deep load after bulges fitted: 31ft 6in.)
Displacement: Deep load as built: 31,150 tons Deep load after bulges fitted: 33,240 tons.

ARMOUR: Lower belt: 13 inches thick from 'A' turret to 'Y' turret, reducing to 4 inches at bow and stern.
Upper belt: 6 inches.
Decks: Forecastle deck: 1 inch.
Upper deck: 1 inch increasing to 1½ inches adjacent to barbettes.
Main deck: 1 inch increasing to 2 inches over magazines and machinery spaces.
2 inches on Glacis.
(At 1922-24 refit, 7ft wide bulges fitted along hull sides extending from 80ft aft of bow to 80ft forward of stern, and at 1934-37 refit additional 4 inch armour fitted over magazines on middle deck, and 2½ inches armour over machinery spaces).
Turrets: Front faces 13in.; sides 11in.; top 4½in.

117

Barbettes: 10 inch reducing to 6 inches at junction of main deck.

Casemates: 6 inches.

Conning tower: 10 inches.

ARMAMENT: (As built): 8-15 inch/42 calibre MK 1 guns in twin turrets.

Max. elevation 20°.

Range: 24,400 yards.

14-6 inch/45 calibre MK XII on single pedestal mountings, 12 inch casemate 2 on superstructure deck.

2-3 inch High angle AA on single pedestal mountings.

4-3 pounder on single pedestal mountings.

4-submerged 21 inch torpedo tubes.

ARMAMENT: (after 1934-37 refit): 8-15 inch/42 calibre MK I guns in twin turrets.

12-6 inch/45 calibre MK XII in casemates.

8-4 inch HA/LA in twin MK XIX mountings.

2-8 barrel 2 pounder MK VI Pom-Poms.

2-Quadruple 0.5 inch MK II machine guns.

4-Above water 21 inch torpedo launchers on upper deck, forward.

MACHINERY: 2 sets Parsons turbines direct drive to 4 shafts. HP turbines to outer shafts, LP turbines to inner shafts.

18 three drum large tube Yarrow boilers with superheaters. Oil fired. Working pressure 250 psi.

Nominal rating: 40,300 shp.

Max. speed: 21.5 knots.

Fuel capacity: 3,400 tons oil.

Range: 4,200 miles at 10 knots.

COMPLEMENT: 997-1,247.

GLOSSARY OF TERMS

Abaft Astern of

Abeam Alongside

Admiralstab German Admiralty High Command during W.W.1

Battlecruiser Fast, heavily armed capital ship designed to act as advance scouting force for battle fleet.

Battleship Heavily protected and heavily armed vessel designed to form part of a battle fleet.

Bulkhead Wall within a ship.

Bulwark Hull side above top deck level.

Casemate gun Gun fitted to protrude from a ship's side.

Conning Tower Armoured emplacement from where a vessel is controlled when in battle.

Contents Gauge Instrument carried by SCUBA diver which indicates quantity of compressed air remaining in his cylinders at any time.

Cordite Propellant for shells fired from guns. Slow (in explosive terms) burning combination of chemicals ignited by detonation of small explosive charge.

Cruiser Fast, lightly armoured warship with medium calibre armament intended to act as scout for main fleet.

Decompression Slow ascent from depth to allow excess of gases within a diver's body tissues to be safely released. In amateur diving, achieved by slow rate of ascent combined with remaining at predetermined depths for an established length of time prior to surfacing.

Deckhead Ceiling within a ship.

Depth Gauge Instrument carried by a diver which indicates the depth of water above him.

Dreadnought Battleship built after 1906 (Britain) or 1908 (Germany) and so called after the first ship of the type, HMS *Dreadnought'*.

Destroyer Small, fast, lightly built British warship for attacking the enemies larger, slower warships principally with torpedoes, and for screening their own fleet's larger warships from submarine attack.

Forefoot Base of a ship's bow.

Foremast The foremost mast of a ship.

Kedge anchor Spare anchor, often used for warping ship. Stern anchor on larger ships.

Knot Nautical mile per hour: about 1.15 miles per hour.

Mainmast	The aftermost mast when referring to ships with two masts.
Port side	Left hand side of a ship when looking forward.
Prow	Top of a ship's bow.
Shotline	Long length of rope with weight attached at one end and buoy to other, used to mark a wreck before diving.
SCUBA	Self Contained Underwater Breathing Apparatus. In the context of this book, compressed air cylinders carried with diver and no attachment to the surface.
Starboard side	Right hand side of a ship when looking forward.
Torpedo Boat	German equivalent of British destroyer.

BIBLIOGRAPHY

Brassey's Naval Annuals			1906-1920
Jane's Fighting Ships			1906-1920
Taschenbuch der Kriegsflotten	*Kapitänleutnant B. Weyer*	J. F. Lehmans Verlag	1918
The Grand Fleet 1914-1916	*Viscount Admiral Jellicoe*	Cassell	1919
Germany's High Seas Fleet in the World War	*Admiral Reinhard Scheer*	Cassell	1920
Scapa and a Camera	*C. W. Burrows*	Country Life Books	1920
Narrative of the Battle of Jutland		HMSO	1924
The Truth about Jutland	*Rear Admiral J. E. T. Harper*	Murray	1927
Death of a Fleet	*Schubert and Gibson*	Hutchinson	1931
Naval Operations of World War 1 (Vol V)	*Corbett and Newbolt*	Longmans Green	1931
The Army and Navy during the Conquest of the Baltic Islands in October 1917	*General Von Tschischwitz*	Command and General School Press (U.S.A.)	1933
Der Seekrieg	*William Wolfslast*	Verlag Ullstein	1938
Jutland	*Captain Donald McIntyre*	Evans Bros.	1957
Black Saturday	*Alexande McKee*	Souvenir Press	1959
Warships of World War 1	*J. M. le Fleming*	Ian Allen	1959
Battleships of the World	*Siegfried Breyer*	Conway	1960
Battle of Jutland	*Geoffrey Bennett*	Batsford	1964
Royal Oak Courts Martial	*Leslie Gardner*	William Blackwood	1965
Yesterday's Deterrent	*Jonathan Steinberg*	McDonald	1965
The Great War at Sea	*Adolph A. Hoeling*	Cassell	1965
The Smoke Screen of Jutland	*Commander J. Irvin*	Kimber	1966
Mutiny on the High Seas	*Daniel Horn*	Rutgers (U.S.A.)	1969
Dictionary of Disasters at Sea during the age of Steam 1824-1972 (2 Volumes)	*Charles Hocking*	Lloyds	1969
Scapa Flow 1919	*Friedrich Ruge*	Ian Allen	1969
Royal Navy Diving Manual		HMSO	1972
Jutland to Junkyard	*S. C. George*	Patrick Stephens	1973
Warships in Profile: B110	*Friedrich Ruge*	Profile Publications	1973
Warships in Profile: König	*Tobias R. Philbin*	Profile Publications	1973
They Called it Accident	*A. Cecil Hampshire*	Kimber	1974
Guns at Sea	*Peter Padfield*	St Martins Press (U.S.A.)	1974
The Phantom of Scapa Flow	*Alexandre Krganoff*	Ian Allen	1974
The Salving of the German Fleet	*J. Pottinger*	Stromness Museum	1975
The Great Liners	*M. Maddocks*	Time Life Books	1978
The Dreadnoughts	*D. Howarth*	Time Life Books	1979
Die Deutschen Kriegschiffe	*H. Hildebrand*	Kohlers Verlag	1980
Luxury Fleet	*Holger H. Herwig*	Allen and Unwin	1980
Nightmare at Scapa Flow	*H. J. Weaver*	Cressrelles	1980
Cruisers	*Bernard Ireland*	Hamlyn	1981
The Grand Scuttle	*Dan van der Vat*	Hodder and Stoughton	1982
This Great Harbour, Scapa Flow	*W. Hewison*	Orkney Press	1985
Jutland	*N. J. M. Campbell*	Conway	1986

OTHER SOURCES

Admiralty Chart No. 35:
   Scapa Flow and Approaches. 1913 edition and later.   MOD (N) Taunton
Admiralty Hydrographic Records.   MOD (N) Taunton
Admiralty Accounts and Papers: CMD 1068: Battle of Jutland, Official Despatches.
Plans of various vessels
Press reports and articles
Personal notes.
Report on Sub-littoral Survey of Scapa Flow: edited by Dr. Frances Dipper
Marine Conservation Society Records.

INDEX